William Vine presenting a copy of his book
'Old Willingdon' to Margaret Goldsmith, the chair of
Willingdon Parish Council, November 1978.

(Photo courtesy of The Eastbourne Gazette)

All profits from this 2020 reprint of this book will be donated to
**Chalk Farm LDC (Learning Disabilities Centre)
run by the local charity E.A.P.A.G.
(Eastbourne Area Parents Action Group).**
https://www.chalkfarmhotel.org/
Registered Charity Number: 1048192

ACKNOWLEDGEMENTS

I should like to express my grateful thanks to those residents as well as those associated and interested in the Village for their help and contributions in my quest for information and materials for this book.

W. J. Vine.

During July 1969 my cousin Cecil Vine had the honour of being granted a family Coat of Arms in recognition of his public service to the village. With this family background it is of little wonder that I have found the collecting and writing of this history to be a labour of love, and I have little doubt that present and future generations of the Vine family will follow the same pattern.

CONTENTS

ILLUSTRATIONS

INTRODUCTION

Why did I get this burning desire to write a history of Old Willingdon? I suppose that primarily my roots are so deep down, here in Willingdon.

Generations of Vine families have lived in this village for over 200 years. From family records and reports, handed down from generation to generation, one finds that throughout the whole of this time they have been either farmers or butchers or, as in the last three previous generations, have been both; throughout this period they have always taken an active and prominent interest in the activities of the Church and Village affairs. Greatly interested in sport especially that of cricket.

From my own recollections my Father and his brother James were, during their life times Choirboys, Choristers, Bellringers, Sidesmen and members of the Parochial Church Council of the Village Church. They also participated in day-to-day Village affairs which resulted in them becoming members as well as Chairman of the Parish Council, Governors of the C of E School and other local committees, and captains of Willingdon Cricket Club.

View of Upper Willingdon, taken from Butts Brow in 1922

OLD WILLINGDON

Originally Willendone and later Wilindon. Bounded on the North by the Parish of Hailsham (which then included Polegate), in the East by Westham, in the South by Eastbourne and East Dean and in the West by Jevington and Folkington.

Looking at the ordnance map dated 1888 one is immediately aware that the original Parish of Willingdon covered a far greater area than that of today, and did in fact stretch to the coast at Langney Point and along to most of the area now covered by Princes Park.

As late as the end of the 1920' s Willingdon was still mostly an agricultural community, with as many as 12 major farms, as well as a number of smaller ones. Several of the larger farms were those belonging to the Ratton Estate, and farmed by tenant farmers – one such farm "Church Farm" being farmed by my father.

Records show that in 1832 the population of this entire parish was 603 persons. Fifty years later it had increased to 794, and one had to wait a further fifty years for it to reach 1,000.

The main part of the Village, in common with so many villages was clustered around the Church. The Church (St Mary-the-Virgin), the vicarage and the Church of England School and School House taking up this central position in the village.

The church is Norman in design; it is built of local stone and flints. The green sandstone rock was quarried from a large quarry which in years gone by, was sited in the vicinity of the Congress Theatre. Proof of its existence has been traced back as far as Roman times. At this site was a small inlet and port, known as Longus Portus (Longport) from which barges transported this stone to points along the coast, where it was used for building purposes.

In most of the towns and villages throughout this area, one has evidence of it, especially in the structure of our churches and noticeably Pevensey Castle.

In our village as in most villages on or close to the South Downs flints were extensively used in the construction of houses, walls, farm buildings as well as for metalling our roads. It is therefore only logical that our village church is built mainly of flints and greenstone rock.

The flints were dug from the extensive beds of flints just below the surface of the turf on the Downs. During my boyhood I vividly remember the teams of horses and carts going up on to the Downs, and returning with the loads of flints, which were dug up with the aid of a large type of gardening fork, the base of which was wider and longer, with the "Tines" much closer together than the ordinary fork so that on lifting the flints from out of the soil the dirt would fall through leaving just the flints on the fork, to then be loaded on to the cart.

Records relating to our Church are available dating back to the 12th century, and an authentic list of the clergy who have been the priest or vicar date to the year 1086, and are displayed on the north wall of the church, adjoining the Vestry. The earliest one recorded being Godfrey the Priest and Note! – and of The Manor, as it was customary in those days for the Lord of the Manor to be responsible for the upkeep of the church. No manor of any standing was not without its own private chapel thus the reason for "and of the Manor".

The history of the church has been extensively and painstakingly unravelled by one of the Church Archivists, namely Professor Harry Berry; but before moving on, and without encroaching on his territory one should just mention further points of interest namely Ratton Chapel in the NE corner of the church. For Latin scholars, historians or to those interested in Heraldry a visit to this chapel will afford much history and information concerning former Lords of the Manor and their close connection with the church. Also within the church The Font dates back to the 14th century and is carved from the local greenstone rock. The clock in the 12th century church tower was installed to commemorate the Golden Jubilee of Queen Victoria in 1887. Taking the path from the Church porch to go round to the churchyard, on the lefthand side of the path approaching the tower one sees the very ancient stone coffin. This was once used as a watering trough at Willingdon Hill Farm. It later, by some means or other, became transported to the stables, cartlodge and granary, which have since been converted into the attractive residence "Marlowe" at 19 Church Street.

During the time that these former farm buildings were tenanted by my father it was still in use as a water trough. On relinquishing his tenancy he contacted the Rev. O.L. Tudor, our vicar at that time, and suggested that something of such historical interest should be preserved. It was agreed that it should be removed to a place which would be more in keeping with its intended use.

With the aid of a wagon and a team of men it was transferred to where we hope will be its final resting place adjacent to the Church.

It is of interest to note that this coffin has been hewn from green sandstone rock which we now have proof has been quarried in Eastbourne dating back to Roman times. It can still be seen in the construction of many of the ancient buildings around this part of Sussex. All of which adds to its present and, will no doubt, add to the future interest shown in it.

Church Bells

In the year 1618 Sir Nicholas Parker, Knight, owner of Ratton Manor gave a large bell to the Village Church.

In the year 1724 it is recorded that 5 bells were made from the metal of the four old ones and inscribed: "Sir William Parker and William Hyland, churchwardens, R. Phelps, Londini Camparius me feat".

The Rev. Henry Hodson D.D. Vicar and Richard Phelps of London made these five bells.

Willingdon Parish Church, before the addition of the clock to commemorate the Golden Jubilee of Queen Victoria in 1887

In 1860 Canon Lowe (Vicar of Willingdon) reports: This autumn the first bell in the peal was re-cast by Messrs. Mears of London at the expense of the Parish, and again in 1875 a new bell was put in the Tower in place of the old third bell which had long been broken. At the same time the other bells were re-hung and put in perfect order by the firm of Messrs. Mears & Stainbrook, Bellfounders of London.

In 1915 the gift of a sixth bell was made by the family of Alexander Wells. A former resident and prominent Churchman. The faculty description read; "A treble Bell for the Tower, by Gillett and Johnson".

In 1933 extensive repairs at a cost of £277 were carried out by Gillett & Johnson. The tenor bell No 5 was cracked as were bells 2 and 4. They were recast at Croydon.

Music and the Church Organ

In the years 1830-1840 Bassoon & Clarinet were used in the Church. These were played by Mr. M. Mockett and Mr. S. Hollobone. At this time it is thought that there might have been a small orchestra, but after this it is known that only a flute was used, and this only had one key. From this James Stevens, the verger, sounded the note to commence the singing.

An American organ was then established by the Rev. O.L. Tudor in 1890. This was in use for the next few years.

A parishioner then records the use of a barrel organ. To arrive at the sacred tune it had first of all to be wound through several peculiar tunes.

Mr. Haylock, organist as well as schoolmaster, fitted a pedal arrangement to the organ. Later there was a harmonium (sold in 1949 for £15).

In 1894 a new organ was purchased at a cost of £550. This was placed where the present War Memorial now stands but removed to the west end of the Church in 1947. In 1950 the manually operated blower was replace by an electrically operated one, then in 1951 the re-conditioned organ was established in the gallery which was constructed for it.

From excavations carried out in the vicinity of the Tower one is led to believe that on the site of our present Church, once stood an even earlier church, or at the least a place of worship, dating back to Saxon times. Willingdon and its surrounding district abounds with proof of the presence, in considerable numbers, of our Saxon forebears. In recent years proof of this was brought to light by the unearthing of the Saxon burial ground at the top of Chalk Pit Hill, In preparation for building the houses which stand on its site and so aptly named "Saxon Place".

Archaeological surveys and digs have also found much evidence of the Saxon presence on the Downs between Willingdon and Jevington and around that area.

Willingdon was, right up until and shortly after the sale and break-up of the Ratton Estate, a closely knit community. Everyone throughout the Village was known to one another at least by name, and it was often jokingly said that many knew far more about you than even you yourself did! No doubt that one of the contributing factors was that it was not until 1920 that we had our first motor bus service, when the Maidstone and District Motor Services started a service from Hastings to Eastbourne via Hailsham, Polegate and Willingdon. Before this date, villagers could only rely on a somewhat unreliable lift to Eastbourne by a seat on Burchett's Horse Bus which came through the Village on Tuesdays and Thursdays. As this was always a gamble as to whether enough spare room was available to squeeze a passenger in amongst the very varied assortment of boxes and parcels which made up its load.

The dice were also loaded against you from the fact that Willingdon was the last point of call on its journey between Herstmonceaux, its starting place, and Eastbourne. The remaining alternative was to walk into Ocklynge and catch a Town bus at the bottom of Cemetery Hill. The hill was at this time considered to be too dangerous for the double decker open top buses to negotiate. One other course to pursue was to hire the local horse and cab, run by that well-known figure, Tommy Stevens, who besides being the local cab proprietor was the village coal and wood merchant, general carrier and hearse proprietor and jobbing builder. So here again the chances were weighed heavily against you, as the cab could be engaged for a wedding or a funeral or the horse that pulled it could be more strenuously engaged in another branch of the business.

A further study of the 1888 ordnance map shows that at that time Hampden Park was not a large enough community to be shown. The railway was, of course, in existence, but was then known as The London, Brighton and South Coast Railway. The station stood on the present site, but was then known as Willingdon Station and was primarily for the use of Ratton House, the Estate and to a lesser extent the inhabitants of Willingdon. Visitors to Ratton were met at the station and transported by carriage to the house. All coal and heavy merchandise came to it by this means, also cattle foods and other farming requisites, which were then transported by horse and cart or farm wagon to their final destination.

I well remember my father and a few farmer friends buying and sharing a railway truckload of coal, delivered to Willingdon Station, there to be unloaded and transported by the customer. The cost of which amounted to £5 per truckload.

As time passed Hampden Park by virtue of its position beside a main-line railway station began to grow, and it was not long before the name-board on the station changed from just WILLINGDON to read Hampden Park (in small lettering) FOR WILLINGDON (in large lettering) and still later on, as it continued to expand a reversal in the size of the lettering took place and at an even later date, with Hampden Park having become a residential area of considerable size the word Willingdon disappeared.

The very attractive popular park as the public now see it, was up until its purchase by the Eastbourne town Council in 1901

"The Decoy" attached to Ratton. From Saxon times onwards every Manor of any note, had its own Decoy, being defined as an area of woodland, with a lake or expanse of water within its boundaries. Its function was to provide water-fowl for the table at the Manor, as well as to provide sport, such as shooting parties for the squire and his guests.

Hence today we have Decoy Drive the main road leading into Hampden Park and skirting the park on its northern side.

On the sale of this, the original Decoy, Lord Willingdon created a new decoy on the opposite side of Decoy drive and slightly north and west of the former one. This is shown on the ordnance map as "The Coppice". Its boundaries being defined as situated at one end by Decoy Drive and at the far end by woodlands Avenue, with a narrow strip of meadowland between it and its boundary with Kings Drive (now, of course, entirely built-up). This, too, like the former decoy covered an area of woodland and a sizeable lake, at the side of which a boat house was built and housed a couple of shallow-draft boats. This decoy was kept up in an excellent state of natural preservation right up to the time of the Ratton Estate sale. It was, of course, fed from the same streams supplying the lake in the park – one from the stream running from the village pump and from the other stream running from the Ratton pond, which was once at the entrance of Walnut Tree Walk and Parkway.

Now after some 50 years of neglect and the take-over by nature one has a hard job to picture it as it was as a former decoy.

We now turn our attention to the farmland on the north side of Decoy Drive. These fields were known as "The Park" no doubt from the fact that it comprised of the Land attached to Park Farm situated in Park Lane, then Park Farm Lane being just a lane connecting the farm with Ratton. The beautiful old Manor House which still stands there was the original Park Farm House with its large duck pond on the opposite side of the lane. The present public house known as "The Parkfield" has without doubt taken its name from these fields which once comprised "The Park". Throughout my lifetime all this land was part of Spots Farm (formerly on the brow of Woodlands Avenue) which took the place of Park Farm when it ceased to function in Park Lane.

Crossing the railway line at Hampden Park and at a distance of some 500 yards due east, one comes to the Hydneye, now a large housing estate, still retaining its original name, as it always has done through the centuries. HYDNEYE at some 500 years past, was a very important town. It was classified a being " A limb of the Cinque Port of Hastings, and remained as such until the year 1287, at which time there were disastrous and unprecedented storms, which at the same time coincided with a slight tilting of the continental shelf resulting in the total destruction of this township, leaving no trace of it whatsoever.

These same storms were also responsible for the destruction of the original town of Winchelsea, which now lies beneath Camber Sands. The few survivors made their way to higher ground to the north west where the existing Winchelsea was eventually built and stands to this very day. At the same time these storms caused the River Rother to change its course, and in consequence instead of entering the sea in the vicinity of Hythe, it now flows into the sea at Rye.

Referring back to Hydneye, it is of interest to note that places with the name ending in "EYE" denoted Islet and in a majority of cases tidal. It is a well known fact that Hydneye, standing on that area of higher ground, was at high tide an Islet, as were the other Hydneyes to be found around this area, such as Court Hydneye, Plough Hydneye, Little Hydneye, and Green Hydneye, all of which were once within the boundaries of the old original Parish of Willingdon.

The whole area around Hydneye and right up through the marsh to as far inland as the outskirts of Hailsham, Magham Down and Herstmonceux were tidal, therefore all of that acreage of fertile grazing land which comprises the marsh was once merely saltings.

It is very obvious what happened to the town of Hydneye. It too shared the same fate as did the original Winchelsea, they were overcome and completely destroyed by the inrush of the sea during the period of those terrible storms, which no doubt had the effect of re-moulding the coastline in many of the low-lying areas, and history tells us that it was not until well in the 1400's that the sea again started to recede.

The old Willingdon Drove used to run from The Hydneye eastwards joining the Stone Cross-Langney road at "Hide Hollow" where the road branches off to Westham and Pevensey. On this corner once stood the old Langney Post Office, which according to a Kelly's Directory of 1882 had its address as Langney P.0. Willingdon, Sussex.

Before proceeding I think that I should halt and define the meaning of "A Drove". This is an unmade-up lane giving access to the fields on either side of it. Before the advent of cattle transporters, all cattle had to be driven from either the nearest railway station yard if having been transported by rail, or otherwise "On the hoof" from A to B. The men who used to drive them were known as "Drovers". They were employed by farmers and cattle dealers for this very purpose, and in order to get them into a specified field, would often have to drive them along the length of a drove to gain access to the particular field. Needless to say, these Drovers had a fantastic knowledge of the countryside; one could almost say "Field by Field".

Owing to the vast housing developments taking place in the Langney area, it is now impossible to follow the course of this original drove, part of which has been re-named "Old Drove". A new, part dual-carriage way road named Willingdon Drove now runs to the south of the old drove from a roundabout in Lottbridge Drove at Hampden Park and emerging at Langney by the side of the large shopping precinct.

To me, being one who knew these droves both Willingdon and Lottbridge Drove, and has actually driven cattle along them to fields which at one time were owned by my father and my uncle, look upon both of these present busy highways as a "misnomer" and indeed a far-off cry from the original cattle droves, often almost impassable during the winter months.

It has at least preserved the name, but I wonder how many of future generations will know what "Drove" alluded to and for what purpose did it serve?

At Langney we are at the eastern boundary of the Old Willingdon Parish and now head in the direction of Langney Point and that section of sea shore which was at one time within the bounds of this large parish. Turning towards Eastbourne we pass St. Anthony's Hill (Its tower now demolished) and on to "The Lodge Inn ' ' where once again Kelly's Directory quotes: "George Wood, licensee, The Lodge Inn, The Crumbles, Willingdon, Sussex," and worthy of note a public house of the same name continues to stand there to this very day.

Continuing along the road towards Seaside, which in 1888 was known, as well as shown, on the ordnance map as EAST WARD. It is now that one passes over the Crumbles Bridge nearby the Queen Alexandra Cottage Homes. This bridge spans a dyke carrying the water from the various ditches on the marsh to the Crumbles Pond and now to Princes Park Lake.

Just beyond this little bridge on your left-hand side is the far end of Lottbridge Drove, running through the marshland between Hampden Park and the far end of Seaside. The Eastbourne Gas Co. works was formerly sited along Lottbridge Drove on what is now part of the large Bird's Eye Factory complex. Here once again the postal address read: "W.A. Darlington, Manager, The Eastbourne Gas Works, Lottbridge Drove, Willingdon".

Beyond the Seaside end of Lottbridge Drove and only a few hundred yards distant one comes to another landmark on the map and still within the parish, that of "Norway Cottages" now dominated by the church of "St. Andrews Norway". This title "Norway" intrigues both residents and visitors alike, but is thought to be a derivation of "Northway" as the road out of this end of the town, on approaching Langney turns north towards Hailsham.

The parish southern boundary from "Norway" turns slightly inland from the coast in a line north of Whitley Road and across Willingdon Levels and then curving towards the Downs at the point of Green Street Farm and embracing all that land under the Downs and shown on the map as "Sheeplands". It was here that the large flocks of sheep, which were at one time such a familiar sight roaming and grazing the Downs were brought during bad weather and during the lambing season. The huge collection of sheep folds all along this stretch of land was just a part of the farming scene.

Over the years our western boundary has remained practically unaltered, with the land of Willingdon Hill Farm stretching out to the edge of East Dean and Friston and at one point approaching Jevington and eventually dropping over the hill to Wannock and the Mill Stream, taking its name from the old watermill which stood at the upper end of the once popular "Old Mill Tea Gardens". For as long as one can remember, the lower course of this stream marked the boundary between the parishes of Willingdon and Polegate until the year 1939, at which time it was thought necessary owing to a reclassification of the ecclesiastical boundaries of the two parishes to move the boundary from the line of the stream to a new line some 300 yards to the south just north of Broad Road.

This new alignment had the effect of placing the Windmill in the Parish of Polegate, so I suppose at last it can now be referred to as Polegate Mill, and not Willingdon Mill under which name it was built and remained as such for so many years.

MEMORIES OF RATTON

RATTON according to Doomsday Book records was originally RADETON (meaning Road town)*. For many centuries the highly respectable family of Parker were the residents and proprietors of Ratton, as can be seen by a visit to Ratton Chapel within the village church of St. Mary the-Virgin where the tomb of the thrice wed Sir Nicholas Parker stands, with his three wives kneeling at his side in postures of reverence and adoration. Much historical knowledge can be gained by a visit and a study of this chapel. It is recorded that Ratton goes back to Saxon times, when it is stated the whole manor was then valued at sixty pounds!

The original Ratton Manor stood on the site of the Home Farm, which since the developer moved in, is now called Ratton Village. The original gate piers of this old Manor can still be found, as at this present day they form the entrance to a private house known as "Winscombe" at 36 Ratton Drive. This was not the main entrance to the Manor, but was that leading into the rear and domestic quarters and outbuildings. The preservation of these gate pillars are such that they are likely to stand for years and years ahead.

Practically all trace of the original manor has completely disappeared. "The Gatehouse" which was mentioned in the Doomsday Book, and restored in 1558 from a most dilapidated state, still stands there today, and kept in an excellent state of preservation. At the rear can still be found relics of the Old Chapel, which goes back to the time when the Monks from the Abbey of Grestein (Normandy) were in residence there after being granted an adjoining parcel of land (The Grove) and the chapel. A legend still exists to this day that these monks planted 12 Yew Trees, known as the 12 Apostles and were said to have put a death curse on any person responsible for their destruction.

---

*RADE-TON This name may have been given in consequence of the British or Roman road running from REGNUM to LEMARIS in Kent and passing through the Parish of Willingdon originally WILLENDONE and later WILLINGDON (as stated in Michell's M.S.).

Ratton, Willingdon

View of "Ratton", the home of Lord and Lady Willingdon. It was completely destroyed by fire in 1940

What I am now going to narrate may be sheer coincidence, but during these last few years, when the developer has been transforming the whole area of Ratton, orders were given to a local firm of tree fellers to remove one of these Yew Trees. This was carried out. Very shortly after this – in a matter of days – the head of the firm unexpectedly and suddenly died. His foreman carried on the firm, and a second Yew Tree was uprooted and destroyed. The foreman was himself suddenly taken ill and died. A little while later the new owner of The Gatehouse had a third Yew Tree uprooted and destroyed; within a fortnight he suffered a heart attack and died. Maybe this is coincidence, or is it? The remaining nine Yew trees now have a preservation order placed on them!

In the earlier part of this book I referred to Godfrey the Priest and of The Manor at the time of 1086. Without doubt he was Priest at the Village Church as well as at this chapel attached to ' 'The Manor' '. Over a great number of years this Manor of which I am now writing, gradually became more and more dilapidated, and a new Ratton was built and was situated 300 to 400 yards westward on the rising ground leading up to Babylon Hill.

This new Ratton was Georgian in design and from the description of it given to me by my father, who knew it well, it must have been a very imposing mansion. He has told me how it was destroyed by fire on Sunday 20th December 1891.

At 5.30 a.m. on that Sunday morning they were roused from their beds by a member of the household going round and waking the villagers, requesting them to proceed as quickly as possible to the scene of the fire to give all assistance they could.

On arrival the menfold immediately formed a bucket chain in an attempt to contain the fire (which had now gained a firm hold), until the arrival of the Fire Brigade from Eastbourne. Eastbourne's 3 fire stations were alerted, but of course in those days some time elapsed before they could arrive on the scene. First of all the horses had to be collected and brought from the various stables to the main Fire Station (this was on the site of the present Public Library in Grove Road) where they were harnessed to "The Steamer" – a type of "Donkey engine where a fire had to be lit in order to get up steam to work the pumping mechanism. Another " Steamer" was kept at the Cavendish Place Fire Station (now the entrance to the yard of M. P. Harris Ltd) where the same procedure had to be gone through. Then at Old Town (Watts Lane) a manual engine was kept. This was the first to arrive on the scene, and although the villagers had done yeoman work with their bucket chain and salvage of furniture and treasures, the fire had now gained an alarming hold.

At this point I am inserting a local newspaper's description of the fire:

"Ratton in Flames" – Sunday 20th December 1891 – The pastoral quiet and orderly routine of the village of Willingdon received a rude shock on Sunday morning by a conflagration of enormous proportions. About half past five, at which time of course it was quite dark, the upper part of Ratton, the residence of Mr. Freeman Thomas J.P. was discovered to be on fire. The Hon Mrs. Thomas (Mother of the young squire) – who was away from home on the occasion, was one of the first to notice the outbreak. She at once called her maid and roused the household. The alarm was given in just the nick of time, as those who had been sleeping in the house had hardly made good their scape when portions of the ceiling fell in and set the rooms in a blaze. Spreading with great rapidity, the fire soon became quite uncontrollable, but no time was lost in communicating with the Eastbourne Fire Brigade.

The manual engine from Old Town arrived first on the scene, but was quickly followed by two Steamers from the Grove Road and Cavendish Place Stations, attended by a full complement of firemen under Capt. James Towner. In fact out of a total of twenty-seven, no fewer than two dozen responded to the call of duty, and of the others two were on the sick list.

By this time it was patent that little could be done to save the premises, which presented the appearance of a huge furnace.

With a view however of saving as much as possible, the brigade set vigorously to work to check and to confine the ravages of the fire, and meanwhile a legion of busy hands were occupied in stripping the lower rooms and removing their contents to a place of security. Thanks to the praiseworthy energy displayed by the villagers and others the bulk of the property was ultimately got out but a good deal of it was unavoidably damaged either by fire or by water.

As the fire increased its hold of the building not-withstanding the herculean exertions of the firemen the spectacle assumed a weird and imposing character and the conspicuous position of Ratton which stands (or rather stood) on the slopes of the Southdowns, in front of a semi-circular plantation and overlooking Eastbourne and the broad expanse of the marshes lying between that town and Hastings and Hailsham, caused the conflagration to be seen for many miles around.

Fortunately there was a good supply of water, the Eastbourne Water company's main extending directly up to Ratton and enabling four jets of water to be simultaneously poured upon the structure.

The fire continued burning up to mid-day, but dense columns of smoke rose from the ruins during the entire day. In addition to the principal furniture most of the pictures, books, plate and jewels were secured. A box containing valuable family deeds was also subsequently found, though it was in a somewhat charred condition.

Not only did the inhabitants of Willingdon turn out en masse to witness the regrettable outbreak, but many hundreds were attracted from Eastbourne particularly in the afternoon, when a crowd of some two thousand had gathered in the vicinity of the mansion. This as may be imagined was finally reduced to a complete ruin, only the outer walls and two or three rooms remaining intact. Supt. Renville of the Hailsham division, and a number of policemen were on duty, but they had no difficulty in preserving order. The damage which is covered by the insurance in the Sun Fire Office is estimated at between £4000 and £5000. Some of the servants had narrow escapes.

The maid of Mrs. Brooks (daughter of Mrs. Thomas) who was staying at Ratton, had only just got outside of her bedroom door, when the ceiling of the room fell in with a crash.

The furniture as it was got out of the mansion was at once removed to Southdown House, an empty building belonging to Mr. Vine, the plate being deposited in Mr. Filder's house.

Mrs. Thomas herself went to Mr. Cooper's house and the servants found a temporary home in different cottages in the Village.

Mr. Freeman Thomas with his butler (Wythe) was away at Catsfield as guest of the Hon. T.A. Brassey at the time the fire broke out at Ratton, but they drove over and arrived a little after two o'clock. Capt. Brand and Mr. Ingram (Agent to Mr. Thomas) drove over and took the Hon Mrs. Thomas back to Glynde. Mr. William Thomas and Colonel Thomas who were staying at Eastbourne visited the scene of the fire during the day.

The wagons in which the furniture was removed were lent by Mr. Cooper (Chalk Farm) and Mr. Fielder (Park Farm). One of Mr. Cooper's milkmen, who lived at Ocklynge, and a man living with him gave the alarm to the Old Town firemen, who were very soon on the road to Ratton with the hose reels. The air in the early morning was bitterly cold, the wheels and other parts of the engine, as well as the hose, being more or less covered with icicles. All night on Sunday a number of firemen remained in charge of the premises, and next day a poodle dog belonging to Mrs. Brook was found among the debris in a charred and very weak state. It should be stated that the fire was confined entirely to Mr. Thomas's residence which is completely detached and a considerable distance from any other structural property.

(End of "Ratton in Flames")

During the day teams of wagons and carts supplied by the local farmers transported the salvaged furniture to Southdown

Park Farm House, "The Old Manor House" in Park Lane

House (Nr. Red Lion Inn) which belonged to Wm. Vine (my grandfather) and was empty at the time, whilst the valuables were taken down to Park Farm House (Park Lane) where lived Mr Filder and his family. He farmed Park Farm which was one of the larger farms of the Ratton Estate.

On the site of this now "Fire Gutted" Georgian Mansion was to arise yet another "Ratton". This one Tudor in design. The building of which was commenced in 1899 and completed during 1901, and which perhaps uncannily suffered the same fate as its predecessor by being completely destroyed by fire during its occupation by the Army in 1940.

This last "Ratton" is the one I remember so well and still have such vivid memories of. It is those which I shall now write about. This beautiful mansion, its lovely grounds, those wonderful walled-in gardens; the influence it had on the way of life in the village; its dependence on the village from which it obtained its labour and vice-versa, the source of employment for many of the inhabitants who were employed variously at the house itself, in the grounds and gardens, on the Estate farms, and on the maintenance of the Estate roads.

Before delving into all this, firstly let us meet the owners, Lord and Lady Willingdon and their two sons Gerard and Inigo. The elder son Gerard was killed during the 1914-1918 war. He with a number of other young men of this village gave their lives to this cause. Their names are recorded on the Memorial in our Church. The second son Inigo therefore became heir to the family title, which he holds today.

Now to Lord Willingdon. Born 1866 died 1941 that most popular and pleasant "Squire" of Willingdon was educated at Eton, during which time he was captain of Eton College Cricket 1st XI. Cricket was one of his joys of life. He played for Sussex County XI, was a member of M.C.C. at "Lords" and his name appears as one of its former Presidents. He was an all round sportsman.

A personal friend of King George V, they often played tennis together, a sport at which the King excelled.

26

Lord Willingdon was a born diplomat as well as being endowed with a pleasing personality. One of his early commissions on behalf of this country was to go out to the Far East to smooth out the difficulties from the aftermath of the Boxer rebellion and to pave the way for future trade. To his credit this mission was most successful. From then on his climb up the diplomatic ladder was further success, step by step culminating in his becoming Viceroy of India in the meantime having been A.D.C. to the Governor of Australia. His other Colonial posts, were those of:

Governor of Bombay 1913-1919
Governor of Madras 1919-1924
Governor of Canada 1926-1931
After his term of duty as Viceroy of India he became Lord Warden of the Cinque Ports 1937-1941.

It is said that behind every successful man there is a woman. Unquestionably that woman was Lady Willingdon, she possessed great strength of character added to which was natural dignity and charm which endeared her to all who knew her. She was at all times her natural self in whatever company she found herself to be in.

She was the daughter of Lord Brassey, who was in politics a staunch Liberal. It is said that when this young man, then Freeman Freeman-Thomas (Later Lord Willingdon) asked for her hand in marriage, Lord Brassey insisted that he changed his politics from that of Conservative to Liberal. In order to win the hand of his "Fair Lady" this he did.

He eventually entered politics as the Liberal M.P. for Bodmin and in the Liberal Government of that time became Liberal Chief Whip.

Both Lord and Lady Willingdon did, of course, take a great interest in the Church and worshipped regularly with members of their family and household in the Ratton Chapel within the church.

The Village School was then Church of England (built in 1853), Lord Willingdon was one of its Governors together with others drawn from the village community. They both prided themselves that they knew every villager by name.

At the Malthouse (now shops just by the Post Office) stood a large old ivy-covered house in part of which lived one of the Ratton employees. Part of this Lord Willingdon had turned into a Reading Room for the use of the menfolk of the village. It contained a library, a billiards table, and around the sides of the room were spaced small tables and chairs for games of dominoes, draughts and cards. One strict rule was gambling in any form was absolutely forbidden.

The Decoy, so much a part of the Ratton scene, referred to in an earlier chapter is worthy of further mention. Having been in existence from Saxon times, it leaves one in little doubt of the importance attached to it by the owners of Ratton since those early days when its primary function was that of a source of food, especially wild fowl.

When Lord Willingdon decided to sell this original decoy to the Borough of Eastbourne to transform into the attractive and popular Park of to-day, he must have decided that a decoy was still an essential feature of his estate with "Ratton" standing in such a commanding position at the foot of the Downs, together with its beautiful gardens, encircled in a Park-like setting. In creating a new decoy on its eastern perimeter it was still in view from the house and its terraces, thus being an added attraction, even though its original function was not so important. The accent now being on its use mainly for pleasure and leisure. Totally unaware at this time that its existence as such was to be so short lived.

Now we return to "Ratton" itself. There were 2 notable annual events on the Ratton calendar, namely The Village Flower Show and the Tenants' Banquet.

The Flower Show was held in "The Combe" a large field just below the house. Although now completely built up the name of this cul-de-sac still brings back memories of that event. This was always a great occasion locally, and was fully supported by all in the village. There were exhibits of Flowers, Fruit, Vegetables, Poultry, Rabbits, and Pets. There were Sports, including Tug-of-wars, Pony and Donkey rides for the children. A band was in attendance and the whole proceedings wound up with a dance in the evening.

The annual Tenants' Banquet was held in the very fine dining-hall at Ratton. Invitations went out to the tenants, farmers on the Estate farms, as well as to the tradesmen connected with it.

Now we turn to the grounds and gardens. They were recognised as being amongst the finest in the district. With Lady Willingdon the gardens and their planning were said to be of paramount importance to her. The cost caused Lord Willingdon considerable financial anxiety over some of those schemes and projects, beautiful as they were when completed.

From the fine terrace at the front of the house there were uninterrupted views looking out over Ratton Bottom (Parkway), the Decoy (The Park) and across to Pevensey on to Hastings and along The Weald of Sussex and Kent.

The main entrance to the house was on the west side facing the Downs, from the drive, one first entered an imposing courtyard. From here leading out on to the Downs and up to "Babylon" was an avenue flanked on either side by a hedge of clipped yews, the path lead on up to the roundel of trees on the crest of the Downs directly above Ratton, and known to this day as Babylon. At the time of which I am writing it was perfectly maintained – a circle of trees with an iron fence surrounding it, with paths running directly east to west and north to south and at their inter -section was a large pile of specially selected large flints dug from the flint beds in the vicinity. It was a recognised fact that had Lord and Lady Willingdon remained at Ratton, this spot was chosen by them to be their resting place – whether this ground had been consecrated in readiness for such an event I have been unable to find out.

I do know this, that at the east entrance was an iron gate that was always kept padlocked, and everyone in the village looked upon it as hallowed ground, and as such no one attempted to put a foot inside it.

Just outside the East Gate was a seat and it was to this spot that Lord and Lady Willingdon often came to enjoy that beautiful view across to the Weald.

Before moving away from Babylon I am sure that it is of interest to mention the "Dew Ponds" which are dotted here and there over the Downs. The dish-shaped ponds constructed primarily as a source of watering the flocks of sheep, which for so many years grazed the Downs and kept the turf almost equal to that of a lawn.

The secret of the construction of these ponds was known only to one ma n. He was engaged by Lord Willingdon to construct one such pond in the Combe just below Ratton House). Every move of its construction was carefully watched and noted by the agent to the Estate, and feeling confident that he was in possession of the "know-how" at a later date it was decided to build a scaled-down model at the foot of Babylon at a spot where one emerged from the yew tree avenue. Every detail was meticulously carried out, but from the time of its construction up to the time of its recent destruction, it was a complete failure in its function as a Dew-pond, whereas the one in the Combe was at all seasons filled with crystal clear water even during a hot dry summer.

It is sad to have to relate that the man, who invented and constructed these ponds, when he died took his secret to his grave without divulging it, although he had sons who could have followed on, so unfortunately, with the passage of time these fascinating dew ponds will gradually disappear from our Downland scene.

Now, after that slight diversion, we will return to our subject and more about the gardens of Ratton.

From the front terrace we face south and pass through the wrought iron gate along the path through the trees, where in springtime the ground beneath them is carpeted with daffodils, and in about 200 yards come to The Grove which was entirely enclosed by high hedges in which there were shrubs and conifers of many species beautifully clipped into the shapes of birds, baskets, pyramids, cones, in fact, in all various shapes and sizes, whilst miniature box hedges defined the pathways. The Grove was a perfect example of the art of Topiary. Here again past memories are kept alive as the road with houses on either side, which now stands on its exact site is known as "The Grove".

Emerging from The Grove one crosses the main drive and enters The Rose Walk , this ran between the two high walled gardens, and as the name suggests was a wide pathway edged with a turf border along either side of the path with a wide border between the turf and the walls. These borders were planted with all kinds of rose bushes, whilst overhead spanning from wall to wall were huge beams covered from one end of the walk to the other by thick wire mesh netting, over this was trained rambler roses, as one can imagine in summer-time this was a blaze of colour.

This path led one from Ratton Drive out on to the Golf Course, the entrance to which was through a small iron gate. As I have just mentioned there were two large walled-in gardens both surrounded by high massive flint walls. These I shall refer to as Garden No. 1. (The lower side of the Rose Walk) and Garden No. 2. (on the upper side). In No. 1 Garden one had all the greenhouses, some heated all the year round and yielding mouth-watering and exotic fruits, whilst around the walls were trained fruit trees, such as peaches, nectarines, cherries, plums and pears according as to what point of the compass they faced. No. 2 Garden had all the soft fruits, such as – raspberries, strawberries, blackcurrants, redcurrants and gooseberries all meticulously netted in, and again with fruit trees trained along the walls. The kitchen garden proper was situated away from this area, outside the main gates and across the main Eastbourne road, its boundaries defined by the similar type of high flint wall as the two upper gardens and running down along the north side of Park Lane and its western boundary along the side of the main A22 Eastbourne Road. These still remain intact today, although now incorporated with the grounds of "Westlords" which was built in 1906.

We now retrace our steps and return to the other side of the road, and at "Winscombe" 36 Ratton Drive, one of the entrances to the old original Ratton Manor which stood on that site for centuries still stands as the entrance to this present day house. The piers still remain as they were all those years ago, sturdy and in a fine state of preservation. This was not the main entrance to the old Manor, but one leading to its rear.

A short distance down the Drive we turn left, and this takes one along to the Home Farm, which was a perfect example of this type of Estate farm. The bell and its small tower at the entrance to the Courtyard still remains. From here the Estate workers were called "To Labour and Off Labour". The ringing of this bell was so punctilious that if the wind was in the right direction we, living in the village, were able to check the time by it.

The Home farm supplied milk, butter, cheese, eggs and cream to the Ratton household. The farmland attached to it covered the whole area of Ratton Bottom from Wish Hill up to the Plantation under Babylon as well as The Combe, and the hill field below Babylon in which the miniature but unsuccessful Dew-pond was constructed.

Ratton Bottom (wherein was the earlier village cricket field) was laid out in a park-like setting with small clump of trees, fenced-in from the cattle, dotted here and there at the far end of which, near the plantation, stood a round flint and stone cattle-byre with a dovecote surmounting its roof – being more ornamental than useful but most attractive. 100 yards distant to the south and 100 yards apart stood 2 stately evergreen oaks which gave this upper end of Ratton Bottom a perfect setting with the curve of the plantation in the background and rising up to Babylon.

From a side-gate leading off of the terrace of the " House" ran a path traversing Ratton Bottom, on up the bank and through the plantation (at about the spot where Melvill Lane now joins

Parkway) and from there in a straight line across the meadows between the Plantation and Butts Lane emerging at the corner of Melvill Lane and Butts Lane.

Like the well-known geometric definition that a straight line is the shortest distance between two points, so was this path, the shortest cut to the village running in a straight line from Ratton House to Butts Lane.

Although used by those at "The House" and tradesmen in the village, it was primarily used by Lord and Lady Willingdon, their family and members of the house hold coming to and going from Church. On fine Sundays it was the usual custom for them all, in the above order, to walk to and from Divine Service, taking up their accustomed positions in the Ratton Chapel within the Church.

This path was kept, like everything connected with Ratton, in meticulous condition, never a weed to be found, its edges trimmed and the "pea" beach, which formed its surface, raked and attended to regularly by a workman of the Estate. Incidentally, another noted Ratton Path was that of the Walnut Tree Walk which was a line of walnut trees stretching from The Home Farm and through the meadow immediately below and terminating at its boundary with Wish Hill which at that time was the main road leading into Eastbourne. Today the road by that name follows that very path that used to run almost beneath those walnut trees.

They were said to have been planted during the reign of Queen Elizabeth the First, but unfortunately over the passage of time, the exact reason or occasion cannot be ascertained.

On occasions when weather conditions did not permit the journey to church on foot, it was then replaced by being driven by carriage and pairs. The family carriage complete with footman as well as coachman.

This was the pattern of life at Ratton up to 12th November 1918 when it and the Estate was split up into various lots and sold by Public Auction. It was a sad day for Willingdon when "The Squire and his Lady" finally said Goodbye. Ratton and its Home Farm passed into the ownership of the Anderson family, a few years later to Mr. and Mrs. Mawhood. Then came the War, during which time it was commandeered by the Canadian Army. It was during their occupation that Ratton, for the second time in its history, was completely gutted by fire, this time never to rise from its ashes.

After the war Ratton was purchased by a Mr. Turner. He then formed the Ratton Estate Company. The ruins of Ratton house were purchased and demolished by the local firm of Builders and Decorators, namely F.J. French & Sons. I feel that this was done for nostalgic more than for business reasons.

Mr. Alan French, head of this village firm, and he himself being a member of an old Willingdon family, and thus having connections with Ratton, business-wise as well as personally throughout most of his lifetime, added to which he took a leading part in village activities, most especially connected with the Church, where during a difficult period he could be said to have been "A Pillar of Strength".

Thus being so much involved with the village and Ratton, I feel that it was only natural for him to want to have the last tangible contact with Ratton. Relics of the house, especially some of the stonework are therefore to be seen dotted about the village, two in particular being the direction stones on the Downs, one on the path from Willingdon to Jevington on the ridge above Butts Brow. The other approaching Willingdon Hill Farm on the path from Old Town to Jevington.

The Ratton Estate Company then sold off the individual properties including those at the entrance gates, those by the gardens and a further one at the middle gateway.

The Home Farm House, plus the conversion of its farm buildings now make up what is known as Ratton Village, with the historic "Gatehouse" close by and now a most attractive private-residence. A walk or a drive around this whole area, makes it apparent that from this once beautiful "Country Seat" has arisen this attractive and highly developed residential district of Ratton and now, of course, within the boundaries of the Borough of Eastbourne.

DURING THE WARS THE GREAT WAR 1914-1918

On the declaration of War many of the young men of the village immediately joined the Forces. Those who were already members of the Territorial and Volunteer units were at once ordered to report to their depots, and were amongst those who formed the spearhead of the now historical Expeditionary Force.

Most of the Willingdon boys joined the Royal Sussex Regiment, which ultimately suffered severe casualties, as the Memorial in our Village Church bears witness to those who gave their lives.

Immediately after the outbreak of war, Willingdon soon became an area of great military activity. Large tented camps were quickly replaced by hutted camps. One massive camp of cavalry and artillery covered several of the fields on the south side and running parallel to 'Church Street. Long lines of stables were erected, being built from a frame-work of timber and covered with canvas.

The main entrance to this camp was exactly where the A22 now runs. One turned in the gateway by the old stone stile which once stood exactly where the traffic bollards now stand on the south side of Church Street crossroads and covered the fields where Friston Avenue now runs and extending east as far as its junction with Willingdon Park Drive.

The village streets (Church Street, Red Lion Street and Coopers Hill) constantly echoed to the ring of horses' hooves and the rumble of army wagons and gun carriages. It was quite a hazardous business being on any of these streets with all the horse-drawn traffic carrying supplies to these large camps because as well as supplying the troops there was also the enormous amount of fodder required for the feeding of all the horses attached to the transport as well as the cavalry and artillery divisions. Many of the heavier wagons were pulled by four-in-hands. The centre shaft had a horse each side of it plus two more trace horses in front, which as you can imagine needed skilful drivers. At this early stage of the 1914-1918 War, one must realise that Motor Transport was only in its infancy and little was to be seen.

The Village Church was taken over by the army on Sunday mornings prior to Matins for the Church service for the troops. Church Parade was quite a spectacle for the local residents and churchgoers. These parades always collected a crowd of onlookers.

Many of the Officers and N.C.O's from the nearby camps were billetted in the village. The Billetting Officer would come around and first of all check your available accommodation, and then allot you with the number which was considered that you could accommodate. My parents who then lived in Church Street were allotted the Chaplain and his wife (Padre Brownlowe). At a later date when they had moved on we had three N.C.O's billetted on us, as ours was a four bedroomed house, and there was just my father, my mother and myself. I can still faintly remember them, two sergeants and a corporal , Sgt. Dawson, Sgt. Welland and Corporal Williams, all from the Durham area. They were awfully nice fellows. The time came, as it did for all these lads to be drafted to France and the various battlefields. One wondered what fate awaited them, did they survive, or were they, too, amongst the victims of that terrible carnage which took place during the four years of that very bloody war.

One great point of interest in and around Willingdon during these war years was, of course, the large Royal Naval Air Station at Lower Willingdon, ironically (as far as Willingdon residents were concerned) named Polegate R.N.A.S. although every square inch of it was well within the boundaries of the Parish of Willingdon. The boundary between Willingdon and Polegate being defined by the Mill Stream, the course of which ran at least 300 yards distant from the most northerly perimeter of the aerodrome. This was no doubt because it was nearer to Polegate than the village of Willingdon, and of course important to it, by the fact that Polegate was a mainline railway station.

The main entrance and guardroom was situated at what is now The Triangle at the junction of Coppice Avenue and Wannock Lane. In fact, Coppice Avenue is built on the very road leading from the guardroom to the two huge hangars which housed the airships. Those hangars stood within the triangle formed by the junction of Coppice Avenue with that part of Broad Road running from that point out to Wannock Lane, which was a secondary entrance to the Air Station and again like Coppice Avenue this section of Broad Road is built on the original Air Station road. It is only in very recent years that the last of the massive concrete blocks which supported the huge girder framework of these large hangars have been demolished. The last ones being in the vicinity of the site of St. Wilfrid's Church.

The Air Station, as one can imagine, covered a huge area. Its boundaries running from the main entrance at Coppice Avenue northwards along the edge of the A22 main London to Eastbourne road to a spot just beyond the present junction with Broad Road and from that point in line due west to the corner of Wannock Lane at its meeting point with the Polegate/Jevington Road; from here it followed the whole length of Wannock Lane until it joined once more with the Coppice Avenue main entrance. One can now envisage the huge area this Air Station covered.

The Sick Quarters were adjoining "The White House' (Willingdon Court) and just beyond was the Officers' mess, with a semi-circular entrance leading in from the main A22 road. Further along at the Broad Road junction, stood a large Radio Station with two tall masts which, in poor visibility, were illuminated by a series of red lights, similar to those which used to outline the roofs of the hangars, these also acted in poor weather as a navigational aid to the airships returning to base from their patrols of the English Channel.

During these war years I, with my parents, lived a "Raylands" 17 Church Street (just below the church and vicarage). From our breakfast room we had an uninterrupted view of the whole Airship Station, with grandstand view of all its activities. At that time Lower Willingdon was little more than a cluster of houses, with just one shop (Hakins Stores) that same little shop, now known as the Lower Willingdon Stores, and one pub "The British Queen", then an old double fronted Georgian house, standing on the same site as the present "B.Q." It was then a little beer house with one of its front rooms serving as a Bar-Parlour. So, as you can well imagine, that between the north side of Church Street we had practically an unobstructed view across to the Air Station and, in fact, far beyond.

The site was closed in 1914, and the Station became operational in July, 1915. It was the major Royal Naval Air Station of the Portsmouth Command. It was equipped with six SS (Sea Scout) type airships, whose duties were to patrol the English Channel from Dungeness to Portland Bill. They had a flying duration of 18 hours. Their function was to seek and attack German U-Boats (or any enemy surface vessels). The U-Boat presence in the Channel was an ever-growing menace to allied shipping. To counter this they carried special type bombs, which worked on the depth charge principle, and they were dropped whenever U-Boats or enemy shipping were identified.

From time to time the airships were fired upon from enemy surface ships. I well remember on two occasions and, being a small boy of 8 or 9 years of age, was very excited at seeing the airships endeavouring to limp back to base with their huge gas envelopes partially deflated, rapidly losing height, and quite obviously not going to be capable of reaching the Airship Station. One made a forced landing in the field (as it then was) just above Melvill Lane. One of the crew slid down the mooring rope to assist helpers who had rushed to the spot. Just as he let go the airship lurched and he fell breaking his ankle. All the same it was safely held down until help arrived from the Air Station which had already been alerted. On another occasion an airship in similar trouble made a forced landing in the Malthouse field, right opposite Chalk Farm Hotel (then the farmhouse) and landed on the exact spot where Tascombe Way is now sited. I was in the garden of our house in Church Street with a boy pal of mine and, as I am sure you can imagine, we were over our garden wall, which backed on to the Malthouse field, and on the spot before it hardly touched the ground. Here again ground crews had already been alerted and were aware of the position of the possible forced landing in this field adjacent to Coopers Hill which, of course, at this time was the main London – Eastbourne road, and they were on the scene within minutes of its touch-down.

In these early days of flying one of the great hazards to flying was, of course, the weather. Navigational aids were few and elementary as was radio communication which at this time was almost entirely confined to messages sent and received in Morse Code, or by visual aids such as the use of an Aldis lamp when visibility permitted or, of course, by compass and map reading.

One of the greatest disasters in the whole history of this important Air Station occurred a few days before Christmas 1917. It was brought about by the rapid and unexpected worsening of the weather conditions. A blanket of fog suddenly swept down through the English Channel and along the coast.

After being grounded by a spell of bad weather making any flying impossible, the weather suddenly improved, consequently all available airships and their crews were launched and set off to patrol the Channel and carry out the object of their missions, namely to attack any enemy shipping which came to their notice.

Alas! during the latter part of the afternoon the fog began to blanket the whole area. Radio messages were exchanged and the five airships then airborne set course for their base at Lower Willingdon, but weather conditions became so bad that it became obvious that this was going to be quite impossible, and the only alternative was to make forced landings where and as quickly as possible.

One of the five airships being in a position nearer to base attempted to get to the Air Station, but before reaching Willingdon conditions had worsened and the crew were unable to find the air field. They eventually made a forced and safe landing in a field on the outskirts of Hailsham. The remaining four were less fortunate. Two force-landed on Beachy Head and the remaining two adjacent to the farm buildings of Willingdon Hill Farm, which was run and farmed in conjunction with Chalk Farm Willingdon and owned by Ernest Smith (I went to school with his son). Willingdon Hill Farm was situated on the top of the Downs halfway between Willingdon and East Dean and in the other direction halfway between Jevington and the Downs Golf Club. In those days there were two cottages at the farm, in one of which lived the Burchett family. Mr Burchett being the foreman-in-charge for Ernest Smith. The crews of these airships decided they would wait here until the fog lifted, but alas Fate decreed otherwise.

As darkness fell, the wind got up and soon the fog began to lift already the Air Station at Lower Willingdon was clear enough for a safe landing to be made, and from here the radio Station sent out the message recalling all its aircraft back to base, where the red lights on the roofs of the hangars as well as those on the wireless masts had been switched on to assist the incoming airships. The two airships moored at Beachy Head immediately got airborne but in the gathering darkness and with patches of quite thick fog still persisting over the Downs they soon lost contact with one another, whereas the two airships moored at Willingdon Hill Farm were still in the process of preparing to become airborne.

One of the two airships which had just left its moorings at Beachy Head, suddenly saw lights through a break in the fog, thinking that he might be over the airfield he came down low to investigate, but tragically it turned out to be the lights at the still moored airship at Willingdon Hill Farm.

Realising his mistake, the pilot put the aircraft into a climb but the hot exhaust from the engine mounted at the back of the gondola ignited the escaping hydrogen from the now torn envelope of the grounded aircraft causing both airborne and the moored aircraft to burst into an immediate blazing inferno.

Crews from the moored aircraft rushed to the now crashed and fiercely burning wreckage, and despite the intense heat and danger of explosion from the bomb load, extricated the dead pilot and pulled the other two badly injured crew members to a place of safety. Having done this, they then fought their way back into the wreckage, and detached the bomb load and carried them with hands already badly burned to a safe distance out of range of the heat.

The pilot (Lt. Watson) of the now burning moored airship, seeing no sign of his two crew members, thinking that they had become trapped in its wreckage without a moment's hesitation rushed into it to investigate, having made sure that no one was trapped within it, he was in the act of getting clear when the bomb-load exploded causing this very brave man severe injuries, including the loss of his right arm. All were at a later date awarded and decorated (I believe by no less a person than King George V) for their acts of bravery. The award being the gold Albert Medal.

One of these crew members and recipient of the award was well known to many of us in the village, having become a friend and frequent visitor at the home of the Richardson family who lived in the end house ("Flint House") of the terrace of houses opposite the entrance to the Church. (It was Harry Richardson, a local jobbing builder, who later gave a considerable amount of both time and skill in the preparation and building of the foundations to our present Willingdon War Memorial Hall.) In the meantime the second moored airship at Willingdon Hill Farm, had been dragged to a safe distance away from the nearby burning wreckage. In this the crew members were assisted by the Burchetts and the occupants of the next door cottage. That night was indelibly imprinted on their minds for the remainder of their lives.

During the time of this catastrophe, the other airship from Beachy Head had landed safely at base. With no other aircraft following on, it soon became apparent to all concerned that somewhere between Beachy Head and Lower Willingdon some disaster had overtaken it, but not knowing to what extent. When news of the tragedy was broken, the village as well as the Air Station was deeply shocked. It has never been forgotten by those of my generation still living in Willingdon, especially when ever "Hill Farm" is mentioned.

I feel that at this point it is fitting to record that during the last year of the war Lieut. Watson (now promoted to Captain) in spite of the loss of his arm in the Hill Farm airship tragedy, returned to the Royal Naval Air Station where he had been serving at that time, now as its Senior Flying Officer.

After the end of the 1914-1918 War, the Air Station was de-requisitioned. Hangars, workshops, administration blocks, living quarters in fact one could say "The Lot" was demolished, of which a large proportion was sectional. All this was auctioned, and for years afterwards they were to be seen dotted around the countryside, especially on farms or where there was a need for outbuildings, all so easily identifiable by their camouflaging, especially on the corrugated steel roofing sheets.

The only original building to survive was the Motor Transport Section Workshops which even now in 1978 can still be seen, now with brickwork replacing what was once corrugated steel panels, otherwise remaining as it was and still on its original site opposite the Free Church at the entrance to Coppice Avenue.

Before closing this saga on this very important war time Royal Naval Air Station, I must record the unofficial and without permission torchlight procession, headed by the Station Band which paraded through both Lower and Upper Willingdon one night, several days in advance of Armistice being declared causing the villagers to rush out of their houses and line the streets, to be jubilantly told by those taking part in the Parade that "The War is Over".

To the consternation of us all the official announcement came some days later, and as a disciplinary measure the Station Commander on this occasion had every man "Confined to Barracks". Obviously some message must have been received that the end was imminent. There is an old but well tried saying of "Never Smoke without Fire".

We, in the village who witnessed this and remember it, always say that we were among the first in the country to get the good tidings that at last the war was over even if it was a little premature and without authority.

For many years after the war, a number of those who served on the Air Station came back to Willingdon, when on holiday, or for a brief visit to keep in touch with local residents, many of whom had become their friends and whose houses had been open to them during those years. We ourselves were one such family where the friendship lasted for many years.

The war over, hostilities ceased and Armistice signed, the village at once put the wheels in motion to decide on what form a Memorial to the dead of this war should take. Meetings were held, suggestions were put forward. One suggestion was quickly agreed upon, that of a Memorial in the Church, upon which should be inscribed all the names of those from this village who gave their lives in the service of their King and Country.

Eventually it was decided that a Memorial Hall should be built and the money to cover its cost collected and donated by the villagers. When erected the Hall should be dedicated to the memory of the fallen as well as a thanks offering for the men who had returned.

Mr. Alister Wedderburn (of "The Hoo") donated the land on the site of the then derelict "Townlands Farm", known locally as "Putlands Farm" named after the Putland family who used to farm it. It was a perfect situation, near the Church and opposite the Village School, (now the Church Hall).

Work on the project was begun in early 1920. Harry Richardson, a local jobbing builder, who lived nearby at "Flint House" (opposite the Church) with the help of his friend Bill "Carrier" Smith from Lower Willingdon set to work demolishing the derelict farm buildings, digging out the footings and building

Church Street, from the point where the A22 now crosses it, showing the former School and the newly errected Memorial Hall

the foundations, which were of considerable proportions owing to the slope of the site away from street level. The building was erected, and a day and time chosen for the opening ceremony.

On Saturday 22nd January, 1921, the Willingdon Memorial Hall was officially opened by the local M.P. Mr. Rupert Gwynne of Wootton Manor (near Polegate). He was accompanied by his wife the Hon. Mrs. Rupert Gwynne. Also on the stage were Mr. Frank Ward (of "Westlords") Chairman of the Memorial Committee, Mr. Alister Wedderburn (donor of the land) accompanied by Mrs. Wedderburn, The Rev. O.L. Tudor (Vicar of Willingdon) and Mrs. Tudor, The Chairman, Mr Frank Ward detailed the steps which had led to the building of the Hall, entirely paid for by voluntary subscription.

Mr. Gwynne, in his speech, heartily congratulated the village on erecting such a fine Hall and went on to say that to do so showed what a fine spirit of unity prevailed in the village, the population of which was, at that time, about 1000 inhabitants.

He then went on to say that the Hall was primarily in memory of the fallen. This fact must never be forgotten either by those present, as well as by those who followed.

On the evening of this memorable day a supper took place for the ex-Service men of the village at which over 80 were present. From this day on everybody became enthusiastic in getting all the various clubs and associations re-organised and the day to day life of the village back to normal. With the new Memorial Hall, dances, whist drives and concerts were organised, greatly appreciated and enthusiastically supported.

From now on more and more houses were being built both in and around Upper and Lower Willingdon. The Village which had changed so little over so many years was now on the threshold of expansion, eventually to grow to the proportions of the highly populated residential area as we see today.

At this time the main Eastbourne-London Road ran straight through the village by way of Wish Hill, Red Lion Street, Coopers Hill and Lower Willingdon.

By now, of course, the ever increasing popularity of the motor car was going forward by leaps and bounds. The village street became snarled up with traffic, especially at week-ends, and could not cope with the ever increasing volume. Char-a-bancs were now becoming a popular form of travel, especially in holiday resorts such as Eastbourne, where it was a "Must" to the holiday maker to take the then very popular trip from Eastbourne, through Willingdon and on to the Wannock Tea Gardens which by now were becoming so well known and popular far and wide.

Voices were being raised throughout the village for action to be taken in connection with this ever growing traffic problem. Meetings were taking place, with the result that representations were made to the East Sussex County Council for the provision of a Willingdon Village By-Pass. This was agreed to, plans were passed, and in a short time its construction commenced and on August 1934 the Willingdon By-Pass was opened. This stretch of road is now known as Eastbourne Road from the Polegate boundary up to the crossing at Church Street and from there on as Willingdon Road into Eastbourne, all part of the A22 London to Eastbourne main road.

On the day of the opening of the By-Pass the village seemed almost eerie in its quietness by the sudden switch of traffic. I well remember the local youngsters organising an impromptu hockey match on roller skates between "The Red Lion" and the Village Pump with little or no interference from traffic.

The opening of the By-Pass seemed to coincide with a spate of development throughout the whole of the Parish, and it continued to grow and grow steadily until the "Second World War" burst upon us in September, 1939. Although the 1914-1918 War had been hailed as being "The War to end all Wars", now in 1939 Hitler had caused it to happen all over again. This time to be on such a gigantic scale never before envisaged.

The reality was brought home to us, when on that memorable September Sunday morning the sirens blared out their first Air Raid Warning, which however proved to be a false alarm, caused by the approach of an unidentified aircraft, which we quickly identified as "ONE OF OURS". Later to become a favourite saying, and one, I might add often expressed with feelings of great relief.

From this moment all the contingency plans were put into operation. The recall of all reservists to their appropriate branch of the armed services, to which a number of the younger men of the village belonged. All the organisations such as Air Raid Precaution Units, the Civil Defence, Auxiliary Fire Service, Ambulance Corps, Special Constabulary, Nursing Auxiliaries, Home Guard, were amongst the foremost to be put on a "War-footing".

How very different a war to that of the former World War this was to prove. From the very first it started off highly mechanised; everything was motorised and it was obvious from the fate of those countries which, had already come under Hitler's "Iron Heel" that the aeroplane was going to play a vital part in the fight for our survival, as well as creating mass destruction both here in England as well as in Europe. In contrast to the 1914-1918 War, Willingdon had no large camps, no Air Station. Being on the coast and so vulnerable to air attacks many of the now empty hotels in Eastbourne were requisitioned by the Government, and used for housing the, members of the Armed Forces. In Willingdon "Ratton" was amongst the first of the larger houses to be commandeered for this purpose and, during its occupation, to be completely destroyed by fire.

During these early days of the War Willingdon was inundated with evacuees from London in anticipation of the expected and eventual bombing. To us here in the country it was almost unbelievable that some of these children had never seen a rabbit running in the wild, some had never even seen a cow and few had never even seen the sea.

It was not long before the authorities realised that this area along the coast was no place to which to bring in evacuees, but one rather to be evacuated, with the growing risk of Hitler's threatened invasion, as well as the danger from frequent attacks from the air, and the almost daily air battles being fought in the skies above us.

During the war years Eastbourne did, in fact, suffer from 104 separate bombing raids, mostly by fighter-bomber aircraft carrying two H.E. bombs on each plane which, having been dropped on the town, they then raked the streets and buildings with cannon and machine-gun fire before turning and, once again, at low level, sweeping out to sea. Sometimes a whole squadron would carry out the raid and on another occasion as few as two individual planes dropping their four bombs would make the attack.

During the autumn of 1940 a notice was posted at the Town Hall, Local Police Stations and prominent points throughout the town advising all non-essential personnel, especially women and children and the elderly, to vacate the town without delay. Thousands moved away, including practically every school in the district. Eastbourne and all around became a ghost area, and later a prohibited area other than to a resident.

At this time the population of Eastbourne fell to less than 10,000. Many residents who were free to do so moved away from Willingdon. The village itself only suffered from the odd bomb usually dropped by enemy bombers which were trying to escape from RAF fighters sent up to intercept them and in an attempt to escape jettisoned their load of bombs regardless of where they might fall. Luckily the majority fell in open country. One such load did however fall on the model farm attached to "Little Ratton" (then a large house, beautiful grounds and a model farm owned by Sir John Lorden).

These killed some of his cows and the remainder of the bombs fell in a line from Little Ratton to the back of Chalk Farm, all luckily missing the village. At night-time the same thing happened when enemy bombers were caught in the beams of the searchlights and became targets for the anti-aircraft batteries or the Mosquito night fighters of the R.A.F.

On one occasion when I was home on leave from the R.A.F., which I joined in 1940, during one of these night raids – which became so frequent that as soon as it got dark, one almost waited for the Air Raid Sirens to give the alarm literally thousands of incendiary bombs were dropped. Once again Willingdon was lucky, some houses in Old Town, Eastbourne were set on fire, but with the efforts of the Fire Service and Civil Defence Corps, as well as the householders themselves armed with stirrup pumps, sand and long handled shovels, all equally highly trained for such an eventuality, had them quickly extinguished. From Old Town once again the remainder fell in a line along the foot of the Downs. A few fell in Wedderburn Road and Butts Lane. These, too, were quickly dealt with and no damage to property was reported.

On three separate occasions when I came home on leave we had windows blown in by blast from bombs dropped close by. Our near neighbours consequently began to look on me as a "Conveyor of Woe" and jokingly, or at least I hoped it was so, would say "Oh dear! he is home on leave again" even when it was a mere weekend pass.

As the war progressed, Army activity in and around Willingdon proportionately grew and grew. The top of the Downs was barred to the public. The whole area between Babylon, Jevington and Willingdon Hill Farm was a tank training ground. It was here that the Churchill tank was put through its paces tested and tried, and when perfected, was inspected by Winston Churchill in person, who was taken up to the top of the Downs to see for himself what this "Wonder Tank" was capable of doing.

It was the Army who first made up Butts Lane from a chalk cart track to a tar-mac road leading on to the top of the Downs and on to this highly secret tank training ground.

The war continued, the Battle of Britain had been won but the Germans' No. 1 Secret Weapon was now to be launched, the "Flying Bomb". Here again Willingdon only suffered from those being shot down before reaching their ultimate target of London.

It was the policy to shoot down the Flying Bomb whilst flying over open country, but unfortunately if a vital hit was not made, then in some instances it carried on for a considerable distance before crashing to the ground, and in these cases often property and sometimes lives suffered.

On one such occasion one fell on Mornings Mill Farm doing considerable damage to the farm buildings, another one fell in the grounds of ' 'The Lodge" (now Lodge Avenue) in Church Street, causing considerable damage.

The occupants of "The Lodge" at this time were Mr. & Mrs. Strange and their family. There were no reports of personal injury at "The Lodge" or from any of the adjoining properties which also suffered considerable damage from the terrific blast.

The bomb fell on a Sunday morning just after 11 a.m when a congregation was assembled in the Church for Matins. The blast struck the Church demolishing the large East window of the chancel and the three South windows of the nave and causing much damage to the roof. Luckily the old heraldic window in Ratton Chapel had been protected and escaped damage. It is recorded that the debris and the shattered glass was cleared sufficiently to allow the Service to be continued to completion. There were no casualties. Other flying bombs fell in open fields and on the Downs within the boundaries of the Parish but causing little or no damage.

The Flying Bomb or V1 as it was officially known was followed by the V2 rocket, to which there was no answer, and caused widespread devastation where ever they fell, London being their target. One of the earliest ever to fall in this country is thought to have fallen in Willingdon, but little was known about it at the time, war-time security was so stringent, and the utmost secrecy was observed.

50

On this particular day a massive explosion occurred, causing a huge crater. This was where Tott Hew Road joins the main A22 road opposite the entrance leading up to Mornings Mill Farm. Luckily this was still open farming land and little damage was caused to the nearest property – Mornings Mill to the NE and the "White House" to the SW, both of which felt the effects of the blast.

The affected area was immediately sealed off. The "Boffins" from the War Ministry were quickly brought to the scene and started investigations. Strange rumours began to circulate the village, one being that a gas main had blown up, another that a bomb had fallen on the gas main, amongst others of a too bizarre nature to even record.

Later it became known that it was one of the earliest of the V2 rockets which for some reason or another was "Off Course" from its main target of London. Continuing up to "V .E. Day" this area saw much military activity, and the skies above were rarely free from the drone of aircraft, laterly very thankfully from our own and allied aircraft.

It was not until after this date that the ban on all but residents and essential personnel was lifted and at long last we could invite our friends to come and visit us.

From this time onwards all awaited the end of hostilities raging in the Far East with Japan, which were eventually brought to a sudden end by the dropping of the atomic bombs on Horishima and Nagasaki, shortly after which "V. J. Day" as announced, and the home-coming of those serving in the forces was eagerly awaited, many accompanied by frustrating and long delays as the machinery of demobilisation took its course often seemingly "Slower than Slow' '.

The pattern now followed a similar one to that at the end of the 1914-1918 War, whereby everyone strived to return to a civilian way of life, and it was not long before the face of the village of Willingdon began to change and grow and grow to the Willingdon we now know and see in this year of 1978. With the obvious comment, time worn though it be, "For Better or for Worse?" The answer is, of course, with the individual.

To many of us who lived here during these times of War the memory of them is still vivid. I am sure the following poem will revive many such memories. Throughout the war years, untiring efforts of many kinds were organised for the benefit of the troops. In the forefront of these was the raising of funds for the British Red Cross Society.

One such effort was the running of a concert in which the following poem was composed and recited by one of our residents, Miss Eva Parris.

Amongst the audience was Major Bird, who became well-known as the founder of Birds Engineering Works at Lower Willingdon.

He was so impressed by this poem that he suggested that it should be printed and then sold, and the proceeds should go to the "Red Cross". This was done and a Great number of them were sold, not only to civilians but also to members of the forces, who carried them with them wherever they went.

It is known that one belonging to Gordon Harris, the son of the local shoemaker, travelled many thousands of miles to many different lands where it was proudly shown and often recited. It ran as follows :.

"Our Village At War"

I'd like to tell you folks a tale About Our Village
Tho' most of you will know it well:
Our Village
But new folks come and old ones go,
And History gets lost, you know,
So listen to "Our Village".

I ought to start with Saxon Days
But you learned all that at school,
Of Smugglers with their crafty ways
Of breaking every rule:
Of "Boney" and Martello Towers
Of Tithe Barns and the rest:

But the tale I'm going to tell you now
Is really much the best.

Not long ago, Invasion came,
You know , "Evacuees" ,
And every home a welcome gave,
And did its best to please;
Our streets were filled with Cockney fun
And how we missed it, when
The order came: "Evacuees, evacuate again" .

Then Regiments of Soldiers came
To thrill the population;
Our Village welcomed all these men,
The stalwarts of the nation.
And when these Scots went marching by
In swinging Kilt arrayed,
Our Village all turned out to see
The smartest Church Parade.

And then these great Canadians came,
Tough guys from way out West,
Defenders of the Homeland, all filled
With eager zest
But bored with nothing much to do –
Just spoiling for a fight;
But can they laugh, and joke and dance?
Oh, Boy! I guess you're right.

And what about our Villagers?
They're not just sitting tight:
There's Home Guard and there's A.R.P.,
Fire Watchers, for the night;
And women doing all they can
To give the First-Aid they're learning;
Their First-Aid Post and Rest Centre
Will keep the Home Fires burning.

The Children, too, are working hard
For Prisoners of War
Each week they have some grand new scheme
For making more and more
They run a Library, sell Chopped Wood,
Give Concerts, for your pleasure;
And if you have not been to one,
Go next time you have leisure.

The Downs, the Fields, the friendly Roads,
They're all part of Our Village;
But most of you will know it well –
This Village
Your Homes, the School, the Village Hall,
The Church Tower watching over all
May Peace dwell in "Our Village".

Eva M. Parris .

THE OLD MAIN ROAD

The Borough of Eastbourne boundary was at the time that I used to go to and from school in Eastbourne (1917-1925) positioned at the top of Chalk Pit Hill, where it remained for a number of years before extending to the bottom of the hill at the junction with Victoria Drive.

At this time Chalk Pit Hill was a steep, narrow hill, steeper than that of today, the reason being that when the present A22 was constructed a deep "dip", in the old road, stretching for some two or three hundred yards towards the village was built up, as one can easily see from the houses now built on both sides of the road.

This original hill had the Chalk Pit on its eastern side, which at this time was an active and bustling lime works. At its entrance, still where it is today, stood three cottages, known appropriately as "Chalk Pit Cottages" now demolished, and on their site stands the buildings of a section of the Eastbourne College of Further Education, whilst further into the pit still stands the two cottages known as "Lime Kiln Cottages". This was, of course, at that time within the Parish of Willingdon, and the children of the families living there had to come to the Village School, the Baldwins, the Clarks and the Fords, and here it is of interest to note that more than fifty years later, one of those schoolboys, Bert Baldwin, still lives at Lime Kiln Cottages, the former home of his parents.

On the west side of this then narrow and steep Chalk Pit Hill was a belt of wood and scrubland, the trees being mostly of May and Ash and the bushes of Sloe. In the days gone by there were, of course, no street lights, one was then heading "Out into the Country" and on our way home from school during the winter months, this stretch of Chalk Pit Hill was always negotiated in record time.

This belt of trees was on the boundary of Ocklynge Farm, one of Willingdon's many farms and was, during the time of which I am writing, farmed by Ernest Smith in conjunction with Chalk Farm. Ocklynge Farm was eventually demolished and now that

Red Lion Street (the part of the London/Eastbourne main road) – Miss Tudor in her early Ford car. In the foreground one sees "The Library" and Venners "Spring Bakery"

and all its farmland is completely covered by streets and streets of houses forming part of the ever growing Eastbourne.

At the foot of Chalk Pit Hill and for some considerable distance skirting Park Avenue all along that bank was a large poultry farm, most beautifully kept and designed with its main buildings on the Chalk Pit Hill frontage and above it a quite large "Ranch type" bungalow.

It was established after the end of the 1914-1918 War by an ex-serviceman and his wife. It was most efficiently run and the hundreds of "White Leghorn" chickens made it a point of interest. It was known as Jack O'Dandy Poultry Farm. It was eventually bought after the death of its, owner Capt. Carlton Williams, by Sir John Lorden at Little Ratton and then incorporated into his extensive grounds and gardens.

Wending our way towards the village one passed the main gateway and drive leading up to Ratton, with the two gatehouse cottages, where . formerly stood, during the period of the earlier Georgian Ratton Manor one single cottage known as "Halfway Cottage", presumably, no doubt, because it was halfway between the village and Eastbourne. The only other nearby dwelling was "Little Ratton" opposite these cottages on the corner of Park Lane or Park Farm Lane as it used to be called. This was the residence of the Agent to the Ratton Estate. On the other corner of Park Lane stood "Westlords" which was not built until 1906. The grounds in which it now stands were up to that time, the kitchen gardens attached to Ratton. The very fine flint built massive wall still to be seen on its Willingdon Road and Park Lane boundaries is similar to the walls which once surrounded the two walled-in gardens and separated by the Rose Walk to which I have referred in the Chapter entitled "Memories of Ratton".

From Ratton gates the road continued up Wish Hill, that same stretch of road as today but narrower, but only the length of the hill was known as "Wish Hill". At the bottom of the hill (now the entrance to Walnut Tree Walk and Parkway) was a large pond surrounded by osiers. In winter-time or times of heavy rain, this pond used to flood and quite often the water from it stretched across and beyond the whole width of the road.

On such occasions anyone walking to or from the village had to await the arrival of a passing horse and cart and request to be ferried across. My parents have recounted that on occasions when no other means of crossing was at hand, menfolk had taken off their boots and socks, rolled up their trouser-legs and carried their womenfolk and families through the flood water.

Besides this pond, in the vicinity there were a number of springs and ponds in the adjacent fields which ultimately found their way into the stream leading into the Coppice (the second Ratton decoy) and on into the Hampden Park Lake (the earlier decoy).

The names of the fields in this area were in keeping with my description of them namely , "The Wish", "The Spring field", "The Pump field" and the "Upper Wish".

The Wish is a derivative of an earlier term – a "Wash" – ·which indicated an area of land abundant with, brooks or marsh-type land. Coming over the hill we come along the road and to the first building at the entrance to the Village Street, "Red Lion Street", this was the Wesleyan Chapel, needless to say that the field alongside it was known locally as the Chapel Field. It was in this field that the now almost forgotten but then very popular "Village treats" were held, consisting of sports, games and feasting, 1n which men, women and children of all ages joined in with great enthusiasm.

The old main road then wended its way along Red Lion Street merging into Coopers Hill at the corner with Church Street and then on down by Chalk Farm to Danns Farm (Portsdown) and so to Lower Willingdon. At this point this section of the old main road became known as "The Lewes Road". · To keep to its original route one has to bear left at the Lower Willingdon Stores into what is now known as The Triangle, where just thisw side of "The British Queen" was situated that well known "Horse Pond" now no longer in existence. At this point the original road kept to the right hand side of The Triangle and joined the A22 at its present outlet by Willingdon Court.

From here onwards its course was the same as the existing road, until getting parallel with the Mill and here bearing left into Clement Lane we are once more on the old original main road and continue on down that steep little hill which was always known as Mocketts Hill, so named after Mockett who was the miller at the mill in its early days. The old once more joins the new where the stream crosses the road by the garage of Polegate Motors – formerly a flint and brick built barn with a slate roof, which was known as Dallaways Barn, this created Willingdon's northern boundary for so very many years.

Before concluding this article on the "Old Main Road" let us briefly look back at its construction and its maintenance.

This main Eastbourne/London road which, before 1934 ran through the village, at the time of my earliest recollection was a flint and mud road and in places quite narrow. When re-surfacing was necessary horses and carts loaded with the local flints from the Downs would bring them to where the road was to be repaired. Here they would be evenly spread over its surf ace, on the top of which would be spread a covering of soil; this would then be watered and steam-rolled until a packed and level surface was acquired. One can well imagine that with such a surface in winter it could become very muddy, and in summer or windy weather very dusty.

Following the flint and mud road, came the tarred surface road. Here a tar bodge was used, which resembled a fatter and shorter version of Stephenson's rocket, with a fire burning under the belly of the bodge to heat and keep the tar in a liquefied state. At the rear was a large tap from which the tar was poured into wide buckets, into these long handled tar brushes were dipped and their contents brushed – or rather smeared over the surface of the road, with a top covering of sand or grit. Incidentally, these early type of tar-bodges had shafts fitted at the front and were pulled from point to point by horses.

More advanced types of tar-bodges took the place of these earlier ones, but still working on the same principle, except that pumps were fitted on each side similar to the principle of the old manual fire engine, and from the tap was fitted a length of flexible hose, at the end of which was a spraying apparatus, which, of course, speeded up the operation considerably, and eventually the shafts and the horse were replaced by a tow-bar and was motor drawn.

The advent of a tar-surfaced road through the village was very favourably received by one and all, less mud less dust, less noise.

Then, no doubt, from County Council level, it was decided to replace the existing surface with one of a more lasting and of a more permanent nature. Consequently a huge "Heath Robinson" type of machinery was assembled in the chalk pit in Butts Lane, which now forms the entrance to Melvill Lane, and from here was produced large quantities of asphalt.

The tar surface was torn up, levelled, and a covering of asphalt was laid down. This was done from boundary to boundary throughout the length of the old main road. As one can imagine it made an excellent surface, but it was proved to have rather serious snags, which no doubt emanated from the method used in its surfacing. The asphalt was brought from the plant, raked to a required depth over the whole road before being steam-rolled with jets of water continuously playing over the roller so as to stop any asphalt adhering to it.

This, of course, left the surface with a smooth and shiny finish to it. This soon proved to be accident prone, as there was no grip for horse vehicle, or car tyre, as now, of course, the car's popularity was growing and growing.

Rain, frost and, of course, falling leaves made it almost a skating rink. The obvious outcome was that this type of road was never replaced, and in its wake followed the concrete road, or the tar-macadam road with its base of large tar-chippings on top of which is laid a covering of fine tar-chippings which can itself be kept in repair by a coating of the time proved spraying of tar plus a top-dressing of chippings, but as a builder says "The perfect house has yet to be built" so the roads of today still have their snags in the form of "chippings".

100 YEARS OF WILLINGDON CRICKET

The word Cricket and Willingdon appear to have been almost synonymous down through the ages. Reports and references both confirm that real enthusiasm for the game goes back as far as the days when the Village XI played in the field in the valley below Ratton House, when this park like setting was known as "Rattan Bottom". On this site now stands the estate of "Parkway". Ratton Bottom and the old pitch, would have been positioned at a point midway along where the road of that name now runs.

Cricket was played here in Ratton Bottom up to the late 1890's under the patronage of the Hon. Mrs. Freeman-Thomas whose son, later to become Lord Willingdon, a former Captain of Eton College Cricket Team took an enthusiastic interest in the village side.

A few years later (during the 1890's) Lord Willingdon had a new cricket field laid out on the other side of the main road into Eastbourne, on the present site of the "Westlords" playing field, now owned by Seeboard.

This cricket ground was maintained at County Ground standards. On the south side of the field an excellent pavilion was erected, whilst on the northern boundary there were seats for spectators (on the present site of the main A22 road approaching the Roundabout).

It was on this field that Willingdon cricket grew from strength to strength under the coaching of the well known Sussex County Cricket Club professional Jesse Hide, who was employed to coach the village side by a local cricket enthusiast, John Jackson, who with his sons "The Cricketing Jacksons" lived at a large house in Church Street known as "The Lawn" now re-named "Hastoun House".

From this coaching emerged the Sussex and England cricketer Joe Vine, one of the four cricketing sons of William Vine, the local butcher and farmer.

His debut for the county was in 1896. He played 879 innings, scoring 24,130 runs including 32 centuries, with a top score of 202. He took 621 wickets at an average of 28.52 each. He represented England on the 1911/12 Australian Tour.

In the test at Sydney he and Frank Woolley created a record 7th wicket partnership of 143 runs. His cricket took him to New Zealand and India. In India he coached the State XI of the Maharaja of Cooch Behar, and then went again to coach the State XI of the Maharaja Jamsahib of Nawanagar (the famous Ranji).

After the 1914/ 1918 War, cricket in Willingdon had to restart from scratch. Westlords no longer remained a cricket field. Cricket enthusiasts in the village rallied under the leadership of Cecil Vine (son of James who was the brother of Joe, and a great name in local cricket). This time the Home Field of Chalk Farm was made available to the reformed Club by Ernest Smith who then owned and farmed Chalk Farm. Cricket flourished here up to the death of E. G. Smith, after which changes took place at Chalk Farm.

P. J. Ellis, owner of the former Hydneye House School later re-named "Hopedene" in Church Street, himself a keen and enthusiastic cricketer came to the Club's rescue by giving the Village XI the use of his lovely (but trifle small) cricket field during the school holidays and at times when available. This was for two seasons the temporary but popular home of Willingdon cricket. In the meantime a search went on to find another cricket field. This time Mr. G. H . Chatfield of Spots Farm came to the Club's rescue.

This field was sited just south of where Friston Avenue now runs. G.H.C. was a great cricket enthusiast as was his son Cecil (known more widely in Eastbourne Amateur Dramatic Society productions).

It was at this ground that Willingdon cricket reached its post-war peak, a second eleven was formed and one had to prove his worth even to get a regular place in that.

The social occasion of the season was the Annual Cricket Club Dance, held in the Memorial Hall. Its success was due to the enthusiasm of, and untiring efforts of the ladies, who provided the refreshments as well as decorating the Hall, which greatly added to the occasion.

Willingdon cricket continued to flourish on the Spots Farm ground until the early 1930s when the President of the Club, Major Aubrey Cole of Hastoun House presented the village with the present Recreation Ground at the corner of Huggetts Lane and the main A22 Eastbourne Road where a special cricket table was laid down to accommodate the cricket pitches, which were kept exclusively for cricket and well apart from the football pitch and games area. Much excellent cricket was played here and one recalls such names as W.W. Wills (Willingdon School Headmaster) J . W. Betteridge (of The Stores) Harry Brett (Head-gardener at "The Hoo" E. Vaughan Tomlinson, Guy Stockwell! which come easily to mind under the captaincy of William Vine (younger brother of Joe). William retired at 55, being top of the batting averages for the season, and from then on became the official umpire to the side. He was followed by his son William James, who took on the captaincy of the side up to the time of joining the R.A.F. shortly after the outbreak of the last war.

Copy of the report of Willingdon Cricket Club Dance (October 1928).

The dance of the Willingdon Cricket Club was held in the Memorial Hall on the evening of October 24th and proved a great success. During the interval for refreshments, Mr. W.W. Wills, Hon. Secretary, gave an interesting account of matches played and the averages of the players, and said that on the whole they had done well having won a fair proportion of matches.

Col. Grimston (President of the Club) thanked the Hon. Secretary for his good work and presented a bat to Mr. Wilfred Wooller for his promising performance as a young batsman.

The ball for the best bowling average was presented to Mr. Walter Morgan, who was congratulated by the Colonel on his record performance.

A vote of thanks to Col. Grimston was proposed by Mr Wills and seconded by Mr. E. J .W. Brown. From then on the Holloway Brothers, Cyril and Roger, took over the reins of the Cricket Club and are still actively connected with it (1978). With their support and advice another generation of cricketers take the field and carry on the tradition of the game.

FOOTNOTE Walter ("Mac") Morgan was recognised as one of the fastest bowlers in local cricket. On more than one occasion he took over 100 wickets during the season.

We can only hope that on this pleasant and excellent ground, as much cricket history will be written in the future as has been done in the past.

Of further cricket interest. On 17th January of last year I had a visit from the younger of the two Jackson sons.

William Dugdale Jackson, now over 90 years of age, who was responsible for my uncle, Joe Vine, becoming a member of the Sussex County Cricket XI. He was on a nostalgic visit to Willingdon after an absence of many years.

He, like his brother George was a keen cricketer, both of whom played on the Westlords ground and were often in the company of the Brothers Vine. Both George and William Jackson when married continued to live in Willingdon for some time. George at the former "Hoo" and William at "Flint House" now "The Five Gables".

WALKING AROUND WILLINGDON

On approaching the old original village from the direction of Eastbourne one passed "Little Ratton" and "Westlords" and the Gate Cottages at the entrance of the main drive leading up to Ratton. The first building one came to on entering the village was the Wesleyan Chapel (now renamed Church). This was built 1n 1894 and it is only in recent years that it has been enlarged to the building which we see today. The original Chapel which consisted of just one main hall can still be easily identified from these newer additions to the building. A well known resident Mrs. A. Stevens was organist at the Chapel for 63 years.

Hard against this Chapel in Spring Terrace stood the village forge, built in 1726 for William Mocket and later run by his son-in-law Robert Russell. It was during his lifetime that I remember it. It was always a hive of activity, as in my boyhood days almost everything was horse drawn, added to which Willingdon was a farming community. It was quite a common occurrence to see four or five horses at a time awaiting their turn to be shod; ranging from the huge "Shire" horses down to a child's pet Shetland pony or donkey. Besides this there were the other activities connected with the daily work of a forge, such as repairs to the iron tyres of wagons and farm carts, repairs to iron ploughs and other farm implements. In the year 1923 Jack Brooker joined Robert Russell and on Robert's death he carried on the forge for Mrs. Russell and eventually became the owner of it and carried on this trade until 1969, by which time the motor had replaced the horse and vast changes had altered the face of Willingdon. What was originally the Russell's private house, standing on the opposite side to the entrance-way to the forge, was first of all converted from the double-fronted Georgian house into a grocer's shop run by Mr. & Mrs. Brooker. This building was later demolished and a modern shop was built on its site.

The old forge continued for a while as a mowing machine repair and re-grinding shop run by the elder of the Brooker sons until this and Spring Terrace, which consisted of a row of cottages facing on to a path leading from the entrance-way to the forge were demolished to make way for the new development.

These cottages had the nickname of "Rabbit Hutch Row" and were known as such throughout the village, no doubt from either the fact of their limited accommodation of two rooms up and two rooms down, with the one and only door leading straight into the front parlour, or by reason of the fact that there always seemed to be a host of children living along this row of cottages.

Adjoining Brooker's shop stood the house named "Wayside" (now embodied in "The Library"). This was at an earlier date a bakery, before Spring Bakery was established. The old ovens could be seen in the lower ground flour until only a few years ago, up to the time that its conversion and inclusion into "The Library" took place.

"The Library" (now a ladies hairdressing salon) was throughout most of its existence the village paper shop and lending library (hence its name), also selling sweets, tobacco and stationery. At the age of five, I with a few other small children attended a small private kindergarten, run by the shop-keeper's wife, Mrs. Lambert. After the Lamberts came the Burgess's to be followed by the West's.

"Papa" West was quite a character, being ex-Navy, an excellent dancer, teaching many in the village, who might otherwise not have had the opportunity to do so. He created much enthusiasm in our village dances. At their retirement it then changed from a paper shop to a chemist's, and a short while afterwards to its present trade as a Ladies Hairdresser.

On the opposite side of the road stood the "Willingdon Lavender & Tea Gardens" which was part of the large gardens of "Hockington House", covering an area now bounded by Wedderburn Road, up as far as "Brydes:' — then the Ratton game-keeper's cottage, before being enlarged and almost rebuilt after the First World War; from "Brydes" its boundary ran in a line parallel to Hockington House. It was run (from 1907) by the Morgan Family, father, mother, 3 sons and 2 daughters. Two of the sons still live in the district. The men used to attend to the market garden and the greenhouses, as well as a greengrocery round by horse and cart twice weekly

The Village Pump, for many years the main source of drinking and domestic water supply to the surrounding cottages

around the village. The womenfolk, in their turn, attended to the flowers and the tea garden.

Hockington House still stands in quite an extensive garden having been modernised but still retaining its original character. It is approached by Hockington Lane, which runs parallel to Wish Hill and emerging at Butts Lane. Facing on to Wish Hill (formerly Red Lion Street) and backing on to Hockington Lane are the four attractive flint and tile cottages known as "Bank Cottages", once part of the Ratton Estate and the homes of some of its employees. The children of one, Robert Parns, still living at No. 93.

Until 1976 these cottages still retained their original numbers 27, 28, 29 and 30 "Bank Cottages", not being numbers given according to the street but by Ratton Estate where each of its buildings was allotted a number according to the Estate Register. Returning to the opposite side of the street, on the site of the flats "Dorchester Court" stood The Spring Bakery, established 1873. In the early part of this century it was run by the Timson Family to be followed by the Venner Family and carried on until 1957 by their son Jack Venner who built it up from a village bakers to the biggest bread and cake business in the district baking many thousands of loaves per week and 16,000 Hot Cross Buns at Easter. Their maroon and gold painted vans were a familiar sight throughout Eastbourne as well as Willingdon and Hampden Park. On the retirement of Mr. Venner, who continued to live in the village, the business was taken over by the firm of Knowles of Worthing, but after a few years closed down. It is obvious that Spring Bakery took the place of the old Bakery which once existed next door, to which I have already referred.

Above the site of "Spring Bakery" and still standing there is the Village Pump which was erected in 1880, built and presented to the village by William Broderick Thomas, up to which date through the centuries it had been a "Dipping Hole" at the source of this always active spring at the base of the Downs. The pump building is constructed of stone, flint and sheeps' knuckle-bones supplied from my grandfather's slaughter-house (opposite 68 the P. O.). There were originally complete panels of knuckle-bones but over the years they have disintegrated and have been replaced by flints.

I can well remember the days when it was part of the daily village scene to see the local menfolk with their wooden hods slung across their shoulders with a bucket attached by a chain to either side going to and from their cottages to the pump to draw the daily requirement of water, which was noted for its pureness and at all times was crystal clear.

People living outside the village were known to come and collect this water in bottles. Along the course of the stream which flowed from the pump to where it is crossed by Upper Kings Drive, were a series of beds of most delicious water-cress. This stream carries on to flow into the lake at Hampden Park, and during times of drought has never been known to cease to flow. A test being during the record hot and dry summer of 1976.

"The Village Pump"

The following information was originally supplied by Lady Willingdon, who had noted the following: An old woman lived near the dell at Willingdon, she had the strange habit of collecting the knuckle-bones of sheep, she collected all the bones she could obtain, and butchers brought them to her. These they sold to her.

In time the old woman collected so many bones that the accumulation was sufficient to build a well, and later a well house, still later a Pump House, was erected and bones were built into the structure by way of ornament." Note: This was obviously before 1880 when the present pump-house was built and, as I have already stated, to conform with the structure of the well house, knuckle-bones were supplied from the local slaughter-house which stood opposite the present Post Office. Thus tracing its history through the ages, it was firstly, just a dipping hole at the spring then a well, later covered by a well-

The former Red Lion Inn prior to 1907

house and finally by a pump-house. The pump now being just a reminder of the past, as the water to the drinking cup is piped in from the mains supply. A somewhat conflicting report regarding the village pump has recently come to light from the contents of an old cardboard box found in the loft of the former home of Augustus Alfred Haylock who was headmaster of the Village School at the end of the last century and the beginning of this present one.

The box was encrusted with the dust of ages but inside were photos, paper cuttings, maps and reports of local "happenings", all of which were in an excellent state of preservation, some of them being at least 100 years old, and others even older.

The article on the Pump was as follows: "Visitors passing through Willingdon no doubt have noticed the "Bone Pump House". In the very early part of the 18th century a couple resided in a cottage (since demolished) behind the present Pump House The Wife sold soup made from ox-heels and used the bones to build a well in her garden. In 1880 William Broderick Thomas Esq. had built the pump house, which he presented to the village. In its gable were his initials and the date, constructed from sheep's knuckle-bones. Others were employed to adorn the walls at each side, all arranged in tiers to complete this unique structure." It is noted that the boy who handed this report to Mr. Haylock was the great-great-grandson of the original soup-maker, who once lived in that small cottage at the rear.

Above the pump and opposite to the Red Lion is "Stream Cottage" which on its south facing wall has an excellent example of boulder work. It is worth noting that in and around this area of the village the word "Spring", "Stream" and "Well" are so evident. Some nearby fields were named "The Well Acres" and today a house in Upper Kings Drive carries that name.

Next to claim our attention is the Red Lion Inn. The original (No. 1) Red Lion was approached through an iron gate and up a garden path. Later a second one was built on the site of the present one, and was a half-timbered building. This No. 2 Red

Lion had a mangle-room attached to it. Here the local women could mangle their washing at one penny (old pence) a time. As well as being a mangling-room it also had the reputation of being the sorting house of all local gossip, and the broadcasting centre of any scandal.

Across the road, on the corner of Upper Kings Drive stood "Southdown House". Originally a three-storey house until its conversion in 1958 when the local planning authority decreed that it should become a two-storey house but retaining all its Georgian features.

At the time of the fire which destroyed the earlier Ratton House on 20th December 1891, Southdown House at that time was empty, and the owner (my grandfather) William Vine made it available for storing a quantity of the furniture salvaged from Ratton.

Overlooking "Southdown" and on the bank opposite, and standing in a considerable amount of ground was "Old Orchard". The entrance to which had been excavated as long ago as prior to the 1914-1918 War, with the intention of building a parade of shops. War came and this never materialised, after which "Old Orchard" was built, but in 1972 on the death of the owner, for whom it was built, it was sold and re-developed for six houses, which have now taken its place.

In the area opposite, now covered by the houses and gardens of "Old Barn Close" stood a cluster of old cottages. Two standing on the site of Yew Tree Cottage, with two more just above, and two separate ones at the rear, as well as the terrace of five called "Garden Terrace" which stood parallel to "The Twitten". It is interesting to note that these were amongst the cottages that drew their daily supply of water from the village pump. They were not demolished until the latter part of the 1960's.

The one remaining cottage is that on the corner of Wish Hill and Old Barn Close, and was at one time said to have been the Police House on the Lewes to Eastbourne turnpike road, and is reputed to be at least 400 years old.

For many years it was the home of the village shoe-maker whose "Snob's Shop" was alongside the cottage. Like so many village tradesmen he was a real craftsman. People came to him from miles around to have their boots and shoes made. His speciality was riding boots. His name was William Pert. He became a local J.P. (1928) serving on the Hailsham Court for some years.

Before "Old Barn Close" was constructed it was the entrance to French & Sons the local builder's yard, which previous to this was a wheel-wright's where the famous Sussex wooden plough was made, and used extensively on the arable land on the Downs in the days when these ploughs were pulled by oxen. My father used to recall the days when oxen were used extensively on these hill farms. Chalk Farm had teams of oxen; he remembers them hauling the wagons as well as the ploughs.

They used to come with the wagons to collect the ploughs from this very wheel-wright's on which my house is now built. In clearing the site prior to building the house, an ox shoe was dug up, it was in perfect condition and I have embodied it in the pier of my entrance gates. An ox shoe on one side and the shoe from a cart horse on the other.

We are now at the Post Office. This was originally a bakery with tea-room. The bakery being in an out-house at the rear. This functioned to around 1940. Only in recent years have the old bread ovens been removed. I can well remember the time when going along "The Twitten" one used to smell the aroma of newly-baked bread, wafting out from the bakery. This building has now been converted into a store-room and a garage attached to the Post Office.

Incidentally, the house called "Twitten Bend" until recently the home of the celebrated radio actress, Gladys Young was, before its re-building into a delightful cottage, the stable, cart lodge and granary. In this used to be housed the pony and specially made small bread-van, used for bread deliveries around the village. This building and its walled-in garden was at this time attached to the Post Office and was its garden.

Opposite the present Post Office and approached by a flight of stone steps is the old house named "Sea View". This was the former butcher's shop being established by the Vine family in the year 1790 although unofficially it was said to be 1764. In its cellars are still to be found relics of those days, such as hooks for hanging up the meat, firmly embedded in the beams.

Alongside the old house stood the slaughter-house and yard. All the meat was home-killed, and came from local markets and farms. One must remember that "Refrigeration" was unheard of even at the early part of this century.

Ice-boxes were extensively used by most butchers. I remember as a child going with my uncle, James Vine, then the local butcher, by horse and cart to the Eastbourne Ice Works in Beach Road, Eastbourne, to collect one hundredweight blocks of ice which were then brought back and placed in huge trays in the "Cold Room" where the sides of beef and other meat were stored.

Local slaughter-houses are now a thing of the past. This is now done from a central abattoir. The disappearance of one more relic of the past.

After the death of my grandfather, William Vine, it was decided to build new premises so, in 1910, the business was transferred to its present position on the corner of Wish Hill and Butts Lane. It remained in the Vine family until 1945, at which date it was taken over by Harry Ingram and now H & J Ingram Ltd.

Now follows an interesting account of my grandfather's wedding: Copied from the report in a Local Newspaper. Willingdon 28th September 1865

Double Wedding

On the 28th ult this village was the scene of gaiety and pleasure on the occasion of the marriage of Mr. Wm. Vine butcher to Miss Mary Fears only daughter of Mr. John Fears, Carpenter and Builder of this parish and of Mr. Joseph Gibson grocer and draper of Barton-on-Humber Lincolnshire to Miss Hagar Vine, sister to Mr. Wm. Vine.

The happy party left the residence of Mr. Wm. Vine about 11 o'clock in three carriages and proceeded to the Parish Church where the ceremony was performed by the vicar The Rev. Canon Thomas Lowe M.A., after which they returned to Mr. Vine's where an elegant breakfast awaited them. To show the esteem and good wishes for the newly married pairs the bells rang merry peals and then garlands were placed across the streets, and flags waved from the house tops and the Church Steeple.

Every poor family in the village and some others in the neighbourhood received a ticket on the previous day, on which was marked the following, a quarter of a pound of tea, one pound of sugar and 2 lbs of good beef without bone, Mr. Gibson giving the tea and sugar and Mr. Vine the meat.

The wedding was well arranged, and all passed off very pleasantly. The happy couples on leaving by different trains for London and for Hastings to spend their honeymoons, received the hearty congratulations and fervent good wishes of their numerous friends.

On the left hand side of the twitten from the Post Office is Pelham Cottage, which during the early part of the last century was a small cottage with a thatched roof which was later replaced by one of slates, at a still later date a modernisation was carried out which included the roof being tiled, which adds to its charm and brings it into line with adjoining properties.

Nearby and still in this Post Office area are modern shop premises built to blend with neighbouring properties, and constructed of flint, brick and tile, on whose very foundations once stood a large ivy-clad house, said to have once been the residence of the village beadle, but in my youth was one of the properties of the Ratton Estate, and the home of one of its employees, Thomas Hollobone and his family, all keen supporters of the village activities.

In the far corner of this house (by the road) was a large through room divided from the house, having a separate porch and entrance. This paved entrance was a favourite spot for the village children to play the then popular game of marbles. This room was the village Reading Room, given by Lord Willingdon for the benefit and recreation of the men of the village.

It was a long room, along its sides were chairs and tables for cards, dominoes and such games, a billiard table stood in the middle of the room, and shelves of books and papers at . the far end. A strict rule was laid down by Lord Willingdon that no gambling of however small a nature was permitted.

In the forecourt of the present Post Office, up to this month of October 1977 stood a large lime tree, laterly with a seat surrounding its base. This tree has had to be removed owing to disease. It was known to the older residents of the village as "The Jubilee Tree' being planted to commemorate the Silver Jubilee of Queen Victoria in 1862.

This being the Silver Jubilee year of Queen Elizabeth II. It is interesting to record that the tree is to be replaced but according to the Borough of Eastbourne Parks and Gardens Superintendent, it has yet to be decided by what type of tree, as the amount of space for its eventual spread has to be considered.

This former tree has now been replaced by an Acer tree. This tree, with a suitable plaque, donated by local residents commemorates the Silver Jubilee of Queen Elizabeth II in 1977.

The next habitation along the village street was the Malthouse Cottages, modernised and built on to in 1972. One of these cottages was for years the original Village Post Office. The old letter box can still be seen in the front wall, as can the brick outline of a low window. My parents have told me from this window to people in the street Post Office business was conducted especially that of boxes and parcels.

On the opposite side of the road, on the NW corner of Butts Lane and the village street stood two very picturesque thatched cottages, at the rear of which was a large yard flanked by stables and out-buildings. Here was conducted the business of coal and wood merchants, local horse-cab, as well as haulage contractor of one Thomas Stevens whose family descendants still live in the village. In the years following the first World War (1914-1918) this was acquired by William Eade and Charles Bridger, who caused a stir in the village by replacing the horse-cab with a taxi, a lorry for the coal, wood and haulage business, and installing a petrol pump on boundary with the main road, which was in those days still the main Eastbourne/London road.

This continued up to the time of the construction of the Willingdon By-Pass (now the present A22) soon after which the business closed down. Bill Eade became Manager of the new petrol station (Crossways) at the roundabout, and Charles Bridger joined Venners the local bakers as a driver and maintenance engineer to their numerous baker's vans. During the next few years these delightful old cottages were demolished to make way for the present development.

Before turning the corner into Church Street one must first move down Coopers Hill to Chalk Farm, which was and still is one of the major farms in the village. For many years it was farmed by a Mr. Paxton, who with his wife and family of three daughters, lived in the original farmhouse (now Chalk Farm Hotel).

Later a young man by the name of Thomas Cooper came as a pupil to learn farming . He married one of the Paxton daughters and later took over the farm on the death of Mr. Paxton. The Coopers took a great interest in village affairs, Chalk Farm House was much in the fore on all the social events and occasions, one being the Willingdon Bonfire Society, which at that time was a strong and active organisation.

On Bonfire Night there was a torchlight procession, headed by the village band, under its band-master and founder the village school head-master, Augustus Haylock. There were tableaux and fancy costumes, which were judged before going on to the bonfire. It concluded its procession around the village by circling the drive in front of Chalk Farm House (a circular drive around a rose garden). From the terrace at the front of the house, judges awarded prizes for the best tableaux and fancy costumes, after which the organisers were invited into the house for "Drinks and Eats".

The memory of the Coopers is perpetuated by the naming of the stretch of road from Church Street corner to the A22 as Coopers Hill. After the Coopers at Chalk Farm came Ernest Smith and his family who carried on in the tradition set by the Coopers. After the death of Ernest Smith, Chalk Farm was eventually acquired by Eastbourne Corporation in whose possession with its satellite farm Willingdon Hill Farm (covering many acres of Downland) still remains.

I, myself, have spent many happy hours at Chalk Farm and in its f arm house in the days of my friendship with the Smith family. We all went to school in Eastbourne the boys at St. Georges in Selwyn Road and the girls at Milton Grange in Arundel Road. In those days we all used to walk to and from Eastbourne to school, there were no buses!

Retracing footsteps to go round to Church Street we pass the flint house at the corner, now known as "The Five Gables", which at the turn of the last century was known appropriately as "Flint House", then the home of one of the cricketing Jacksons. It was he, William Dugdale Jackson, who was responsible for the introduction of my uncle, Joseph Vine, to the Sussex County Cricket Club for whom he played throughout his Sussex and England cricket career. "Flint House" eventually changed hands and was bought by Alexander Wells, a great churchman and Vicar's church warden for 38 years (1900-1938). Twenty-nine of them during the time that the Rev. O.L. Tudor was Vicar of Willingdon. Throughout the years that Mr. & Mrs. Wells lived at the now re-named "Five Gables" they took a keen interest in the village and its day to day affairs. On the death of Alexander Wells, Mrs. Wells presented the Village Church with a sixth bell, in memory of her late husband, who had worked so hard for and derived so much pleasure from his connections with the Church.

Mrs. Wells continued to live at the "Five Gables" up to the time of her death, when the house was bought by Mr. & Mrs. John Paine who run it as a School of English Language for Foreign Students.

No doubt of interest is the fact that the present "Wheatsheaf Inn" Car Park opposite the Inn was originally the Coach House and stables of firstly "Flint House" and later "The Five Gables". The change from "Carriage and Pair" to Motor Car came about during the lifetime of Mr. & Mrs. Well, after which it was bought as a garage and parking space for the Inn.

We now come round the corner into Church Street and to the Wheatsheaf Inn itself. Local history records that originally on this site stood two small cottages, which were later converted into a typical village beer-house, and as such it remained for a number of years. During its early days it encouraged but little trade, so little that the "Man of the House" was, during the day, obliged to seek some alternative employment to eke out a living.

In 1913 a Mr. and Mrs. Cuthbert arrived to take over the Inn. They were a delightful couple, and to encourage them in their task of raising the standard of this little beer-house its owners, The Star Brewery, allowed them to live there rent free for the first year.

From then on The Wheatsheaf progressed, always spotlessly clean, no undesirable would-be customers were allowed over its threshold.

The Cuthberts raised a family of two sons and two daughters, all were highly respected.

The Inn remained in the family until the tragic death from leukaemia of their son-in-law, who had succeeded them as its licensee, ending the family tenancy in 1955.

The building remained outwardly the same for a number of years. The lower half of the building had an unusual facing of green glazed tiles, or more precisely green glazed brickettes. During 1934 a well-known builder, Herbert Compton, carried out an excellent conversion by building an oak timbered "Tudor" type facade which covered the existing outer wall. This conformed with other re-built Star Brewery properties in this area.

It was at this time that a full license was obtained, after which its already growing popularity continued to increase, from time to time it has undergone various alterations and additions to cope with its popularity in this every expanding Willing don.

Just above and adjoining the Inn and on the site of the present two flats, stood a quaint little sweet shop by the name of Dick Martin's, which was run by his wife, known and referred to by the village lads as "Orf", having been christened Orpha. To enter the shop, where once inside the total capacity for customers was three or perhaps four, and this at a squeeze, one first had to go through a gateway on the upper side, go up four steps and enter by a stable-type door, on the inner side of which was attached a large cow, bell attached to a spring, and created enough noise to almost awaken the dead. This bell used to summon Mrs. Martin, or her daughter, Bertha, from the inner depths of the house to the counter, often probably to a child with a farthing or a ha' penny to spend. The farthing would buy an everlasting strip – which was a strip of chewy toffee-like concoction, or for a ha'penny one could buy strips of Spanish liquorice, or a liquorice sweet in the shape of the then popular clay pipe, or aniseed balls at so many per penny and so on up the scale, as well as cigarettes "Woodbines" at two pence for a packet of five, or " Park Drive" at fivepence for 10.

At the rear of the house were long single storey out-houses, which previously were used as a bakery – not as a bakery as we now know it – but purely for the purpose of cooking private orders, such as cakes and pies for private households. My parents have told me that it was quite common for the person concerned to prepare the mix and then send it along to any such bakery to be baked.

Eventually Dick Martin's sweet shop – to many a child's sorrow – was replaced by a grocer's shop, some of the house being incorporated into the shop, having a double fronted window with the entrance at street level fronting Church Street. For some years this was run by G. Boswell and his son. Later changing over to a shoe-maker and repairers and run by Alfred Harris up to the time of being demolished to make way for the present flats.

Between Dick Martin's sweet shop and the Church Street end of the Twitten stood a row of 4 cottages, known as Queen Annes Terrace. The front doors opened direct on to the Village Street straight from their sitting-rooms. These were at first floor level. They were three storeys high, the ground floor being below street level, the back doors of which opened to their gardens, which one can visualize when looking at the present gardens as they are in the shape of a pit, which is exactly what it was in earlier days. It used to be a marl-pit and was known locally as "Battimers Hole" which name was still in existence and referred to as such during my school-days. The cottage nearest to the Twitten was occupied by one "Tailor" Martin – no doubt to distinguish him from the other Martins in the village. Here he applied his trade, and in the summer months his front door would often be open. His front room was his work-room and one could see him busily at work when passing by.

On the opposite side of Church Street on the present site of Nos. 3 to 13 Church Street and prior to 1904 stood two old thatched cottages, in the upper one of these two lived Mr. and Mrs. Joe Read and family, whose descendants still live in and around Willingdon and rank next to the Vine families as its longest residing inhabitants.

At No. 15 Church Street (now the site of the houses known as The Croft) stood the home of Edmund Catt and family. At the entrance of the drive leading up to their old Georgian house stood a very old Sussex style house in the traditional brick and hanging tile of that period. During its latter years it was converted into offices. Edmund Catt was the Clerk to the various Parish Councils which came under the jurisdiction of the area covered by the then Hailsham Rural District Council; from these offices their administration was carried out. The old house eventually

Church Street prior to 1904, showing Dick Martin's sweet shop, also Queen Anne's Terrace, and the thatched cottages opposite

became unsafe and uninhabitable and a danger to passers-by as its south facing wall was flush with the pavement.

The administration of the various Parish Councils, which had been dealt with at this old house for many years, was now transferred to offices at the Rural District Council premises at Hailsham, but still carried out by Edmund Catt, later to be handed down from father to son. Following the move to Hailsham, after the old house had already partly collapsed, it was then completely demolished.

Above and adjoining the Catt residence, and prior to 1913, stood a large cattle yard roofed-in on three sides to afford shelter for the animals, alongside this, just above the yard, stood other farm buildings comprising flint and brick built stables, cart lodge, over the top of which was a large granary all of which belonged to the Wedderburn Estate, from whom my father bought the cattle yard and built a house on its site. This was our home for the next 25 years. The other buildings were bought by Herbert Compton, a well-known local builder, who bought them from their owners The Wedderburn Estate, and during 1933 converted them into a delightful residence which he named "Marlowe" as much of the oak incorporated in it came from the house of Christopher Marlowe (Shakespeare's tutor) who lived at Canterbury, where today we have the Marlowe Theatre to commemorate this famous man. The cattle yard and the other buildings were no doubt those remaining from the original Church Farm before its transfer to the far end of Church Street, to which I later refer. This was farmed by my father.

Just across the road in close proximity to the church stood Church Farm House still being occupied by the former tenant of Church Farm until the beginning of this century. At a later date it was re-named St . Wilfreds, then incorporated into "The Hoo" as the housekeeper's residence and then again in recent years returned to its original status as a private residence, and now after full restoration and modernisation is known as "Coombe House".

The present Betteridge Stores and adjoining ladies hairdressers were originally the coach-house, stables and granary of "The Hoo" and later to be garage and stables with the granary converted into a flat above them. The stores were originally on the opposite side of the road for many years under the name of Hutching's Stores. Alfred Hutchings, being a notable and much respected figure in the village and village life, especially in connection with the church and school.

From the original house and shop, after an intensive conversion, one now sees the attractive residence known as "Old Place".

Before the advent of the shop, on this site stood four cottages, which during the last century were converted into the grocery and general stores catering for both men and womens' complete outfitters and tailoring as well as boots and shoes. It was a large rambling old building being in the shape of an inverted "T". The house on the left and the shop longwise and being on two floors, groceries downstairs and tailoring etc. upstairs. Its trading covered the village and beyond. Deliveries were made in Willingdon, Polegate and Jevington.

The stables, cart-lodge, granary and warehouse composed of 3 storeys, was across the road standing back from it and hard alongside the west wall of the vicarage now converted into a private residence. The ground floor is converted into the entrance and garages, otherwise its structure remains virtually unchanged.

We now come to what is considered the "Hub" of most villages, the Vicarage, the Church and the School, and here we have them together and in that order. So much of village life centred round or emanated from here.

The previous vicarage was a rambling old Georgian House covered by dense creeper and partly screened from the road by large Yew Trees. Two vicars of note since the middle of the last century, who were part of and so much concerned with the village and the spiritual needs of its inhabitants, were the Rev. Canon

Thomas Lowe, 1850 until 1887, a most popular figure and one who took an energetic interest in village as well as church affairs.

Canon Lowe was followed by the Reverend Owen Letchmere Tudor M.A. who must have ranked as one of the most kindly vicars that this Parish has yet known. This was the man whom I and my family knew so well during his 41 years of ministry here in Willingdon (1888 until 1929). Throughout the whole of this time he was a much-loved vicar and, together with his family, highly respected by all who came into contact with them.

O.L.T. was a great lover of cricket and was to be seen, if only for a short while, at most of the "Home" fixtures of the Willingdon Cricket Club. This interest stemming from the fact that he himself, in his younger days, was a Cambridge Cricket "Blue" . The Tudor's had a family of four sons and one daughter. The sons, like their father, were all excellent cricketers. It is interesting to note that recently on 3rd August, 1977, the obituary notice of the last surviving member of the family was announced, that of Brigadier C.L. Tudor C.B.E., M .C. at the age of 88 years.

Mrs. Tudor assisted by her daughter, Miss Brenda Tudor, took a great interest in the Womens' Organisations connected either with the village or more especially with the Church and supported them in person, giving help and advice whenever requested.

With the Tudor family lived Mrs. Tudor's aunt, Miss Maria Jane Campbell, who in her latter years was often to be seen about the village in her rather special Bath-Chair. This Bath-chair was made available for the use of elderly or incapacitated members of the community.

For instance if "Granny" was to be taken out to tea or to visit another member of the family elsewhere in the village, then a request for the loan of Miss Campbell's Bath-chair was made, and, if available, never refused.

This, of course, was a golden opportunity for a bit of "Skylarking" by the younger generation. Young Tommy or some junior member of the family who were borrowing the chair would be sent to the

Vicarage to collect it. As you can imagine on the way he would inevitably be met, or be seen, by one of his pals which resulted that after getting out of sight of the Vicarage a series of free rides would be undertaken, often perilous to the passenger or to any passer-by, and if found out chastisement for the culprits.

One must realize that at this time means of transport was almost entirely by the horse-drawn variety, so Miss Campbell's Bath-Chair was to be frequently seen trundling the Grannies or whosoever required it, to their respective destinations.

From these recollections you will have concluded that the Vicarage, in this then quite small and compact village of Willingdon played a great part in the community's daily life, invariably connected with parochial matters taking place, some of which, being of a festive nature as this cutting from a local newspaper, obviously printed around the turn of this last century, shows. It reads:-

Willingdon Choir Supper

Our Church Choir had its annual supper at the Vicarage a few days ago, and a very pleasant evening was spent. The Church wardens and other principal inhabitants joined the men at the supper table, and afterwards the whole party, with several ladies who kindly attended, adjourned to the Vicarage kitchen, where the time passed happily until a little past midnight, enlivened by various speeches, songs and glees. The glees sung by the choir were much admired, not the least so being the quaint old and now almost forgotten Sussex song of "The Husbandman".

A principal feature of the evening was the presentation of a pair of handsome candlesticks to Mr. and Mrs. Haylock, the excellent head-master and mistress of the schools. The candlesticks were a spontaneous gift from the parents of the children attending the schools, as a mark of their sense of the skill, and especially the kindness with which they have carried out their work for the last four years. The Vicar and Mr Seymour together made the presentation, and the former while explaining that the present emanated solely from the parents, took occasion to remark that, though the gift was necessarily made to Mr. and Mrs. Haylock, who were responsible for the conduct of the whole school, yet equal credit was due in her own departments to Mrs. Hunt, who has charge of the infants.

This remark was well received by the company and Mr Haylock returned hearty thanks for the testimonial which was so totally unexpected by him and his wife, the secret having been so well kept.

Before passing on to the Church one should record that the present Vicarage was built in 1933 but to some of us who knew the earlier one so well are inclined to think that this present one does not seem to have the character or atmosphere of its predecessor, which was at the time beyond restoration.

From the Vicarage we come to our Village Church – the Church of St. Mary-the-Virgin. I have dealt with the church in general terms in the early part of this book. I would not dare to venture into the mass of history connected with it as this has most painstakingly and thoroughly been dealt with by Professor Harry Berry, who has unearthed, interpreted and deciphered so much of its history that has been there over the centuries, but had meant little to the many who were not learned enough to understand the many Latin, Greek or even some of the old English inscriptions and manuscripts. These have now been brought up to date and are together with other church records, and can be read and understood by all who wish to do so, thanks to Harry Berry and our present archivist, Miss Blundell.

Adjoining the church was, as one would expect, the Village School, as in those days it was a church of England School and continued as such until education was taken over by the State. Children came to it from far afield, as the original Parish covered a much wider area.

The governing body consisted of the Vicar and elected members of the village community all of whom served for a given period. Over the years many names of prominent and well-known residents appeared on the records.

For many years Augustus Haylock was its Headmaster. He and Mrs. Haylock took an intense interest in the school and its pupils, as well as taking an active part in village affairs.

Over a period of more than 42 years many of their later pupils were the children of their former pupils. He was appointed Headmaster in 1881 and retired in 1923.

On retirement they spent the remainder of their lives in Church Street and not far from the school. They derived great joy from being among, and in the company, of their former pupils.

Another Headmaster who left his mark was Walter W. Wills, so many had cause to be grateful to both Mr. and Mrs. Wills for their personal kindnesses as well as the desire they showed that nothing should be left undone in furthering their education and moulding their characters. W.W. Wills was a great sportsman, a good cricketer, footballer and football referee. In his retirement he became a bowls player of some repute. One of his hobbies was that of painting in water-colours. His various paintings of local scenes especially the one of Chalk Farm and the Downs are still to be seen in the homes of his friends and relations. He also gave much time and support to furthering the aims and work of the local Royal British Legion.

On his retirement he was succeeded by Mr. Jack Morrall who took part in the transition from Church of England School to that of State School This took place in November 1952. A new school was built at Lower Willingdon and the old Church of England School then became the Church Hall, and the Headmaster's house attached to it became the Verger's residence.

Mr. and Mrs. Morrall, like some of their predecessors on retirement, still live in the village. They take an active interest in local affairs and activities which include organising events for the benefit of various charities.

Retracing our steps, opposite the Vicarage is a large and imposing house named "The Hoo". The word "Hoo" is Saxon and denotes a spur or ridge running out from or being a continuation of, The Downs, and it is on such a formation, at the foot of The Downs, that this house is built. This reference to the Saxon Age again reminds us of their former presence in and around all this area. The old Georgian farmhouse, bearing the same name was sold by its former owners to Alexander Wedderburn Q.C. a rich Scotsman, and eminent barrister and one who helped in the editing of the works of Ruskin. (Hence we now have Ruskin Road which originally was partially within the beautiful grounds and gardens of "The Hoo").

This old original "Hoo" when it was still the Georgian farmhouse was described to me by a former well-known resident. The last surviving brother of the family of "Cricketing Jacksons", who is now a sprightly and very mentally alert 92 years of age.

It was his brother who lived at this former "Hoo" prior to its sale. It was from him that I was given the following description:-

A typical double-fronted old Georgian house, standing slightly back from the road from which it was approached by a wide flag stone path running from its gate on Church Street and leading up to the front door, on either side of this path was a perfectly kept lawn, each with well kept rose beds.

Before the Jacksons it was the home of the Long family who moved at that time to Selmeston. During their stay at the "Hoo" they had to contend with a family crisis. Their daughter was being taught to ride horseback and was being taught and given riding lessons by one of the staff by the name of Pearce who was in charge of the stables and lived in one of the cottages where now stands Hockington House Pearse was taken ill so the riding lessons were taken over by his son. This blossomed into a secret romance, culminating in the young couple eloping. The parents decided to have nothing to do with their daughter but after a while relented and decided to trace their whereabouts. They eventually found them living quite happily and young Pearce working on a farm where they had a cottage in West Sussex. All was forgiven and the Longs set the couple up with a farm. From then on they never looked back. They raised a family (I believe it was three) all sons, who were exceptionally brainy, and later studied law and became barristers.

On the purchase of the original Hoo, its new owner Alexander Wedderburn called in a young and "Up and Coming" architect by the name of Lutyens (later to become the celebrated Sir Edward Lutyens) who was responsible for the design and planning of the present "Hoo" the exterior of which still remains unaltered. The beauty of the house I consider to be that of its south facing elevation looking over its terraces and gardens skirted by two gazebos with steps sweeping down alongside an attractive flint wall. These led to the spacious gardens, tennis courts orchards, hot-houses with semi-tropical plants and fruits, below which were the vegetable gardens whose boundaries were, what is now Upper Kings Drive and Ruskin Road.

Lutyens was assisted in the design and laying-out of these beautiful gardens by a Miss Gertrlude Jekyll whose artistic flair was responsible for the terracing, its walls, the Gazebos, the steps leading down to the lower gardens, the lily ponds along the base of the wall recessed by arches.

Before moving away from these gardens one must comment on the glorious views from their terraces, which were, at one time, uninterrupted. One could stand on the terrace and look along the line of the Downs beyond Ratton to Beachy Head and then along the coast with Hastings in the far distance.

The Wedderburn family exerted considerable influence on the village and its affairs, especially any development around the close proximity of "The Hoo". I have already drawn attention to the stables and coach-house on the site of the present Bettridge Stores. From here one would see the emergence of the coach and pair, the coachman and footman in full livery, with cockades on their top hats, which sported a gold band around them as did their livery.

After the death of Mrs. Wedderburn and ill-health overtook Mr. Wedderburn, their married daughter Peggy and her husband Stuart De la Rue (Chairman of De la Rue Ltd. and also chairman of the original Bentley Car Company) took up residence at "The Hoo". The Bentley cars, 2 sports models and one specially built saloon for the use of Mr. Wedderburn. During the time of the De la Rue's residence, eight gardeners were kept fully employed looking after the grounds and gardens as well as the two large hot-houses and adjoining greenhouse, under the eagle eye of the head gardener, Harry Brett. There is no doubt that during these years The Hoo gardens were second to none throughout the village, except for those of "Ratton".

Unhappily, Stuart De la Rue, a popular person to all who knew him or had contact with him, died at a comparatively early age. Mrs. De la Rue and family left "The Hoo" and for a while her brother Alister Melvill Wedderburn K.C. took up residence, but eventually moved back to London.

For a short time "Clovelly Keppleston" Ladies College moved from its position on the Eastbourne Seafront (now the flats by that name) and took over "The Hoo" under their Headmistress, Miss Frances Brown, who conducted it on lavish lines, and among her pupils were a number from notable families from both here and abroad, but after a few years, when on the retirement of Miss Brown, it ceased to continue, having not met with the success which was anticipated on its move out to Willingdon.

During 1936 " The Hoo" was bought by Col. Marden who moved to it from Halland, near Uckfield, with their family. They lived there up to the time of the death of Colonel Marden.

In 1955 a development company was its next purchaser. The house itself was converted into a series of flats and the remainder of the grounds and gardens redeveloped in the pleasant way in which we see it today.

Before moving away from "The Hoo", of special interest is the large flint building nearby. Stone-lined and flint filled and near the eaves carved in one of the stones is the date 1611. A further interesting point is that the flints are not only knapped but are also square cut. It is the only building in Willingdon so constructed. To find similar construction one must go to

View looking towards The Church and "The Hoo" from Butts Lane and just discernable "Hutchings Stores" (taken prior to 1910)

Compton Place, Eastbourne, the former home of the Duke of Devonshire, or to Glyn de Place at Glynde, which bears out the belief that it was originally an important dwelling. Proof of this can be seen from part of the stone framed window now built up and partly obscured by the boulder built cottages built hard up to its eastern boundary wall and carrying the date 1758.

In later years this building was used as a barn, after at one time being the communal corn store, used by the farmers in the district, because let us not for get that as recently as 50 years ago Willingdon was entirely a farming community. It was never a tithe barn for the church as some less informed people would have us believe.

During 1934-36 it was renovated from the Hoo fruit, vegetable and general garden store, to become part of the Ladies College to which I have already referred. Now, since the redevelopment of "The Hoo" it has turned full-circle and is once more a delightful and attractive residence.

Opposite the Church one's attention is drawn to the fine examples of flint and boulder construction of the six cottages standing there. Two of boulder construction and four of flint. The first flint cottage (next to the archway, No. 32) was, for many years, the Village Police Station wherein was its own jail, complete with iron-barred window and door.

During my childhood there was always great excitement among us when it became known that there was an occupant of the "Lock-Up". The horse-drawn "Black Maria" used to arrive from Hailsham (the local police H.Q.)., The driver being perched up on a high seat at the front wearing the special high flat-topped peaked cap, which these police drivers then wore.

Agog with excitement we would watch the "Prisoner" being bundled into the Black Maria, escorted by a policeman and driven off to face whatever charge had been made against him and answerable at the Hailsham Magistrates' Court. These cottages have now been restored and modernised, being completed during 1975.

Between the flint cottages opposite the church and the Memorial Hall are two semi-detached houses. At the first one named "The Orchard No. 4" lived the Seymour family, Mr. and Mrs. Sampson Seymour and their four daughters, again another one of those families so closely connected and involved with the day-to-day life of the village.

John Sampson Seymour, to give him his full names but known to all his friends and acquaintances as "Sampson", carried on a business in a large workshop (only recently demolished) situated at the rear of the gardens of these two houses and approached through the gateway which still exists next to the Memorial Hall, the business of – and here I quote from Kelly's Directory of 1882 – "Seymour & Marchant. Builders, Contractors, Undertakers, Wheelwrights, Painters and Glaziers" . Throughout this book I have stressed what a closely knit and inter-dependent community this village used to be.

Here again it is interesting to note a further example. It was in this workshop that all the coffins were made for the village's departed and, according to reports from my father, some of the more ornate ones, were an example of fine craftsmanship, which was characteristic of any work undertaken by Sampson Seymour. Here again a funeral in the village involved as well as the coffin-maker, Tommy Stevens, who we have already met, he supplied the hearse and the horse and cab – all suitably decked in black crepe – and Alan French, of F.J . French and Sons, who organised the funeral arrangements and led its procession through the village to the Church.

Mr. & Mrs. Seymour and their daughters were closely connected .to anything concerning the Village Church and all worked untiringly for anything connected with it. Notably, Sampson Seymour who during his lifetime was a choirboy, head chorister, captain of the bell-ringers as well as a sidesman. Kate and Rose Seymour were both school teachers at the village C of E school. Rose later becoming Headmistress of the Hampden Park Infants School. She and a younger sister were accomplished organists and were always available for Church Services ,Weddings, or Funerals when Mr. Haylock (the school Headmaster) and regular organist was not available .

After the death of Mr. & Mrs. Seymour Senr., two of the sisters continued to live at "Orchard Cottage" and were later joined by a widowed sister and it was here, close to the Church and the School which had played such a big part in then lives, that they ended their days having contributed much to both Church and School, and one could say the Village Community as a whole. Willingdon had so many families who were worthy of this kind of mention.

Next to the farm buildings and now almost exactly where the traffic island of the Church Street crossing of the A22 stands was the well known and well used stone stile from which paths radiated to connect with Hampden Park Railway Station, the Park, and another out to the main road into Eastbourne at Westlords. Whilst on the other side of Church Street to the corresponding stile against the school playground wall three paths converged from Lower Willingdon and Polegate – Willingdon being completely surrounded by farmlands. Here next to this latter stile and gateway leading into the vicarage field, shown on the ordnance maps under its correct name "The Hanty" stood the village pound, in which stray cattle were impounded until claimed by their owners. There was at one time, without doubt also a field connected with this village pound, as nearby (at the rear of the cottages opposite the church) stands Poundfield Cottage, recently modernised but outwardly looking little different as originally. This cottage has been the home of the Thorpe family, to my knowledge, for three generations, and is still the home of a member of the family.

We now move along Church Street to the site of the present Lodge Avenue. Until quite recent years all the area of this housing development was occupied by a fine old Georgian house standing in these spacious grounds. Throughout its history it has been known as, Buckingham Lodge, then Sussex Lodge, still later "The Lodge" and finally, White Lodge, up to the

The once familiar landmark "The Old Stone Stile" which before 1934 stood at the present intersection of Church Street and the A22.

time the developer moved in. It was for many years the home of the Raleigh family who were direct descendants of Sir Walter Raleigh. It is of interest to note that Mrs. Raleigh lived to be 102 years of age and in her latter years lived in Ratton Drive.

Some 50 yards distant on the opposite side of the road stands Elm Tree Cottage. This was at one time the village dairy and was run by two brothers by the name of Read, Jack Read the elder of the two, living at Elm Tree Cottage. The archway leading into the neighbouring house "Timbers" together with its garage was part of the original cart-shed and buildings attached to the dairy. Before the Read Bros. it was a private residence and now, after complete restoration, is once more a delightful and distinctive private residence.

Again crossing Church Street and a little further on, one comes to the entrance leading to "Hastoun House", now the Wealden Council's Home for the Elderly, which until purchased by the Council was one of the village's "Large Houses". When John Jackson ("The Cricketing Jacksons") lived there at the end of the last century (1888) it was known as "The Lawn". Its next owners were the Howards, to be followed by Stuart Brodie and family, a popular and well liked man – not one of the world's best drivers of a motor car. With no buses yet on the road, he was always willing to give anybody a lift. On one occasion he pulled up and offered a well known resident, who was equally well known for her lack of tact, a lift into Eastbourne, and received the reply "Thank you very much, Sir, but I would prefer to walk" which amused him greatly and he would tell against himself. On another occasion, a General Election day, he was giving his services to the Conservative Party to bring elderly members of the Party to the Polling Station at the Village School. My father was on duty as a Teller at the door when up rolls a car load of voters in Mr. Brodie's car. My father, knowing everybody in the village and quite aware as to which Party they belonged, said to him, "Who sent you to collect that load, they are the opposition!" His reply was – "Oh! I saw them struggling up from Lower Willingdon, so I turned around and gave them a lift," and he waited and took them back. That was typical of Stuart

Brodie. At this period the name of "The Lawn" had been changed to "Shortlands".

After the death of this popular resident its new owner was Major Aubrey Cole, who was reputed to be a very wealthy man. He bought the adjoining property "Hopedene" had it demolished and its quite extensive grounds added to those of "Shortlands", which he had now re-named Hastoun House. He took a great interest in village affairs and its people and contributed generously to many worthy causes, notably the Church, the School, the British Legion and the most generous gift of all, that of giving the excellent recreation ground on the corner of the A22 and Huggetts Lane as an outright gift to the village and its residents for all time.

Let us now return to "Hopedene" and look back to its functions and its happenings, before its demolition and inclusion into the grounds of "Hastoun House". "Hopedene" stood in the area of ground between the upper entrance to "Hastoun House" and the boundary with "Bredon" on the far side. A semi-circular drive swept in from Church Street, of which firstly one came to the courtyard, with its gymnasium and various other ancillary buildings, centrally situated on the driveway was the rather imposing three storey house, which was formerly the home of "Hydney House Preparatory School" under the Headmastership of Mr. C. W. Norman. It was here that the four sons of the Rev. O.L. Tudor commenced their schooling. On the death of Mr. Norman, the assistant Headmaster, Mr. Maltby, took charge, and within the next few years it became necessary to find larger premises to cope with its increasing popularity .

Hydneye House was mainly a boarding school. A new site for the school, with more spacious accommodation and playing fields, was found at Baldslow near Battle and at the end of 1918 it was to there that the school moved and I believe is still there at present. Here was another change in the village scene. No longer were the hunting-pink school caps with the motive H.H.S. in silver thread to be seen around the village or at the Church Services.

The new purchaser of the school was a Mr. P. J. Ellis, who re-named it "Hopedene" and under this title continued it as a "Cram" School, specialising in a standard of education which, hopefully, would gain its students entry into a University, notably Oxford or Cambridge.

This college, it had now become known as Hopedene College, progressed and went on from strength to strength and gained for itself high reputation, both abroad as well as at home. Among its foreign students, at one time, were relatives of the Japanese Royal Family. They were very popular with the locals, especially the youngest one who was always referred to as "Ashie". His name, or one of his names, being Ashimoto something or other.

He, and either his brother or cousin – I cannot now remember their exact relationship – became keen and quite useful cricketers and represented the College XI in the matches played on the somewhat small, but excellent, playing-field on the other side of the road. In size I would say it was about 150 yards square, and on its Church Street boundary was skirted by a white-painted iron fence, with its cricket pavilion on its boundary backing on to the land adjoining "Elm Tree Cottage". Much enjoyable cricket was played here, as recounted in the chapter describing Willingdon cricket.

P. J. Ellis, built for his and his family's occupation the adjoining house "Bredon" which itself at that time had spacious grounds plus a paddock at the rear. In recent years "'Bredon" has undergone extensive alterations.

Just below on the site now occupied by the house "Fairlight" stood Church Farm, which for a number of years up to the time of its sale in 1922, was farmed by my father. The Loose-Boxes for stabling the horses, together with adjoining out-houses fronting on to Church Street still stand there at this present time. On the bank on the side of the road just above the farm entrance once stood the village stocks. These, in their last stages of dilapidation, I can just remember – What a primitive and uncivilised form of punishment these must have been! Opposite the farm gates stood "Rippingtons".

Then a farm and a farmhouse, all by that name, now just the house stands there. Years ago it was a thatched Shepherd's cot, at a later date enlarged but still thatched to house the Mewett family, who farmed the adjoining farm and farmlands.

Over the intervening years the house has been further enlarged and modernised but retaining much of the original. For many years the old fire insurance plaque could be seen on the wall above the front door. In the event of a fire this had to be rescued from the debris to certify that the building was insured. The plaque has now disappeared. Today they have become a valuable collector's piece, and are much sought after.

Part of Rippingtons farm buildings, especially the old boulder-built barn, form the imposing residence "Adams Barn" and, again, the original Rippingtons stables and cart-lodge converted into "Barn Cottage".

At the far end of Church Street on the righthand side stands the house "New Place" which was built for two sisters, the Misses Overton, in the years just before World War One. This house won an award in an Ideal Homes Competition. Like "The Hoo" the most attractive features are those at the south side and cannot be seen from the road. New Place was designed by the well-known architect John D. Clark of Eastbourne, who lived in Willingdon for a number of years, and with his wife and two sons first lived at Danns Farm House (now Portsdown) and later at St. Wilfreds (re-named "Combe House") in Church Street.

John D. Clark also designed "Field Place" nearby in Huggetts Lane. This was in the Indian style, having been built for Judge Mumford who had served for many years in India and then retired to Willingdon, where his brother-in-law and his sister (Mrs Stretton of Adams Barn) were living.

At this point was the original junction of Church Street, Huggetts Lane and the old Broderick Road, part of which can still be seen where it forms the front boundary to the house on the far corner named "Elmhyrst". The old Broderick Road was originally one of the Ratton Estate roads, and like all of the Estate roads was constructed of a foundation of chalk, a covering of flints, both obtained from the chalk pits and the flint beds on the Downs, plus a covering of beach collected from the Crumbles. This old Broderick Road connected Church Street with Hampden Park for the great majority of the way the present road still keeps to that original road.

Up to the time of the sale of the Ratton Estate after which it became an unadopted road (in the early 1920's) it was a much used thoroughfare, so much so that at the junction of Church Street and Coopers Hill (then the main Eastbourne-London _ road) there was a sign-post pointing up Church Street, with the lettering "HAMPDEN PARK $1^1/_2$ miles". This sign post was only removed when Broderick Road became overgrown and almost un-negotiable after the demise of the Ratton Estate.

From the far end of Church Street we now turn left into Huggetts Lane which at this period was little more than a narrow, country lane, leading to the various farms and again keeping to its original route, to its present junction with the A22, giving access to Hamlands Farm and the farmland on either side, as well as the small adjoining farm, farmed by the brothers Read in connection with the village dairy at "Elm Tree Cottage".

At the bottom of the little hill leading down from the junction with Church Street and known locally as Pidden Well Hill – which no doubt throughout the years had come about by being a derivation of Pidgeon Well Hill, at the bottom of which turning sharply to the right one entered an even narrower lane known as "Jordans Lane" which led to Jordans Farm (Records dating back to 1625) and on down to Broderickland Farm. All this area is now covered by a vast building estate.

When one looks at the old 1922 photo of the small compact village of Willingdon with nothing but open countryside all around it; then today go up to Butts Brow and look at the present view; the change that has taken place and the extensive built up area which now covers it, to me, seems almost unbelievable.

Re-tracing our footsteps we turn from Church Street into Coopers Hill, passing Chalk Farm towards Lower Willingdon, with high hedges and farmlands on both ,sides of the road we come first to the house known as "The Mount" (No. 58 Coopers Hill) which was a small farm comprising of about six fields, farmed by a Mr. Durrant, more as a hobby than serious farming.

A few yards below "The Mount" and at the rear of The Service Station there is a flight of stone steps still to be seen against the bank. There used to be a stile at the top of them which led to a much used footpath leading from Lower Willingdon to the church, or to the stone stile opposite the school as already mentioned. One hundred yards down the road on the lefthand side is "Portsdown" originally Dann's Farm House with the farm and farm buildings alongside it. Here again all the farm land has been built upon, the farmhouse and all the farm buildings have undergone conversion and it is now hard to picture it as it used to be. Here the "Wind of Change" has certainly created a transformation in the past eighty years from the time when my father was farming it, as his first farm when a young man.

In this area were two other small farms. Just below "Portsdown" one comes to Meachants Lane (one of the old bridle lanes) and now leading in to Meachants Court, where once stood a terrace of six old cottages built of flint, brick and slate roofs, backing on to the stream which flowed almost by their backyards, and eventually flowing into the horse-pond just this side of the British Queen Inn.

Above them on the lefthand side of the lane stood I Meachants Farm, whose Farm House still remains, having undergone a face lift, whilst on the opposite side of the lane stood "Marshams Farm", of which there is now no trace.

Here used to work one of the village characters, eventually managing it when the owner died, leaving his widow to carry on the farm. His name was Freddie Hobden, a most likeable and friendly character and known around the village as "Flickie". One of his duties was to run a milk round in the village (in opposition to the Read Brothers). He was a terrific talker, and one of his sayings as he was about to turn for home was – "Well I'd better be getting back and flick around a bit" – hence the nickname of Flickie. It was a usual thing to find his horse and cart tethered to the Jubilee Tree outside of Willingdon Post Office at 10 o'clock at night. Flickie would be doing his "Afternoon" milk round after milking the cows, cleaning out the cow stalls and bedding the animals down for the night. On a winters night, Freddie would set course on his round. One would hear his milk can together with pint and a half-pint measure jangling at its side as he made his way from horse and cart to the house in question, and on his approach one would hear his melodious voice sing out "Hello, Hello, Hello! Here we are again." I suppose to awake any of his customers who might have fallen asleep whilst awaiting his arrival. Even so at this late hour he was ready to draw up a chair and have a chat, and then off he would go hurricane lantern in one hand and milk can and measures in the other.

On one such late night sortie, one of his customers remarked "Have you to wash your churns and cans after you get back home?" His somewhat laconic reply was: "I expect I shall just have to smear 'em around a bit." This got repeated and, as was usual found its way around the village, and in consequence Freddie's "Afternoon" delivery from then on was known throughout the village as "Smear' ems midnight delivery" .

At that time such episodes were all part of village life and from which much amusement was derived.

Retracing our steps along Meachants Lane to the Main Road, and here I must record that from Church Street corner to Dann's Farm (Portsdown) it was Coopers Hill and from there onwards it was always ref erred to as the Lewes Road.

Just beyond the junction of Gorringe Valley Road and now a builder's yard were the stables and yard of a haulage business belonging to one J. Read. His horses and carts were a familiar sight throughout the village as under contract to the then Hailsham Rural District Council he was responsible for the transporting of the road making and repairing materials from the Northern boundary at Polegate to the southern boundary with Eastbourne. He was mostly concerned with the haulage of loads of flints, from the flint beds on the Downs to the location on the roads where they were then steam-rolled in, which then made up the construction of the majority of our roads. On the opposite side of the road was the market gardens, glasshouses and ancillary buildings of Harvey & Son who had greengrocer's shops in Eastbourne. Walter Harvey, its proprietor, a tall and well-known figure, was a great walker. He used to walk almost daily to and from these Market Gardens to his main shop in Gildredge Road (almost opposite the Eastbourne Railway Station).

Continuing down the road, across to the left-hand side, one comes to the Lower Willingdon Stores, which for many years was the only shop in that small community and alongside it on the site of the present garage stood a wheelwright's shop, which at the time of which I am writing, approximately 50 to 60 years ago, was run by one Thomas Taylor, a well known local figure and said to be an outstanding craftsman, who had the reputation of "Take it to Tom" and he would either repair or re-make it for you.

His speciality was the building of handmade farm carts and farm wagons. My father had a farm wagon made by Tom and the craftsmanship was superb. He was a great reader and had a great knowledge of the Bible, of which he had strong views, and it was not an uncommon sight to see him and our vicar, Rev. Tudor, in deep conversation over their sometimes differing views on some aspect of religion.

We are now almost at the "British Queen Inn", but just before reaching it one comes to the Horse Pond, very necessary and always in great demand during the days of mostly horse-drawn traffic. This was the point where the stream which flowed down from Meachants Farm took a right handed turn to pass under the main road (by the Triangle). Its flow was interrupted at the side of the road to enter a man-made trough at almost ground level, oblong in construction at least about 20 feet in length by about 5 feet In width and about 2 feet deep, with a slight indenture in the centre of the outside wall, which by the flow of the stream always kept it full, but allowed it to continue unabated on its course to join up with other streams on their way to the Marsh.

The driver would drive his horse or horse and cart off the road down into the trough going in on one side of the culvert where it passed under the road and on his way out passing through the bed of the stream and on to the road again on the other side. As one can imagine it was an exciting day when a circus came through on its way to Eastbourne, with everything connected with it being hauled by horses, even the elephants travelling on foot.

As the news spread through the village that the circus was about to pass through, the children used to make haste to the Horse Pond (as did some of the grown-ups, too) because it was here that a halt was made and the horses were watered and given the chance to take a breather, whilst this quite lengthy operation took place, before continuing the hard haul of the trailers carrying tents, equipment and animal cages etc, up the hill to Upper Willingdon and on through the village and into Eastbourne.

From the children's point of view the party piece was when the elephants were brought down to the pond after the horses had been re-harnessed to the trailers and were again on their way. It was then that one was wise to stand well back from the pond, as after drinking, they decided that a shower bath was a necessary thing, and water was spurted and thrown in all directions regardless of consequences.

We have now reached "The British Queen". This was originally just a small beer house. A double-fronted Georgian type house. The main entrance to the pub was by way of the front door and into the room on the right-hand side, which acted as the bar parlour, with wooden forms around the sides and, in one corner, a hatchway, through which the beer was served.

At one time during its history old deeds show that it changed ownership for the sum of £46.

"The White House" at Lower Willingdon. The former home of Brigadier S. B. Grimston and family (now Willingdon Court)

Between the last two World Wars, the owners (the Measy family) sold it to the Star Brewery, Eastbourne, who then demolished it and had built the rather attractive and imposing "Pub" which we see there today, and like other Star Brewery Pubs, which were given similar treatment, were re-built by Herbert Compton who was an expert in buildings of that style and architecture.

This area of Lower Willingdon is now known as The Triangle the pattern of roads making it obvious. The portion from the Lower Willingdon Stores and bearing round to the right before again joining the A22 is a remnant of the old original main road. Many years ago this area around The Triangle was known as Foulride Cross because as it implies it was a Cross-roads of some importance. To this point also came the Bridle Way, which can still be traced through the archway under the Railway east of Polegate Station, across to Morning Mill Farm down between it and Willows Farm and out to the A22 from there it followed the route of Tott Hew Road along to Foulride Cross. In years gone by this was a much used link by travellers on horse as well as by foot when metalled roads were few and far between.

Along the parade of shops now at The Triangle is the Butcher's shop. Even now one glance shows that it was originally another of those double-fronted Georgian houses. For many years it was the Lower Willingdon Laundry and was run by a Mrs. Gearing. A few yards further on at the point where The Triangle joins the main A22 road stands Willingdon Court. The whole of this site was previously the house, grounds and orchard of The White House, the home for many years of Brigadier and Mrs. S.B. Grimston and family.

After a distinguished career in the Army, Brigadier Grims ton, who was a brother of Mrs Brenda Tudor (our Vicar's wife) on his retirement in 1919 returned from India to rejoin his wife and family who had returned in 1915. He took a great interest in local and village affairs. He became a Member of the Parish Council, President of the local British Legion and President

Willingdon Mill now known as Polgate Mill. The former Isolation Hospital is in the background

108

of the Willingdon Cricket Club. He was still carrying out these duties at the time of his death in 1928.

They had a son, George, and a daughter, Frances. George was educated at Winchester where he became Captain of the College 1st XI cricket team. Like his father he, too, had a distinguished Army career. During this time he played cricket for the Army, also for Sussex County C.C. later during his retirement he was for a while Secretary to the club.

Frances Grimston, their daughter, was a charming and delightful girl. Her Christian names were Frances Nina, whilst those of her mother were Nina Frances and from a copy of the Parish Church magazine dated November, 1928, under the heading of "Baptisms", the following announcement is recorded – 'October 9th . Nina Frances daughter of Donald Adrian Wallace and Frances Nina Thesiger (Thesiger being her married name). This was a family tradition where the first daughter of the family reversed her Mother's Christian names.

After the death of Brigadier Grimston, his widow gave much of her time to local affairs. She became a member of the Hailsham R.D.C. Took over the Presidency of Willingdon C.C. as well as that of the local Women's Section of the British Legion and, for a period, was President of the Willingdon Women's Institute. She died in 1958. It was then that the White House and formerly Mornings Mill Farm House was demolished.

At the time of which I am now writing (the early 1920's) there were no houses along either side of the main road between The White House and the windmill, from the entrance to Mornings Mill Farm up to almost this point was open land. This was known as Foulride Green, and it certainly lived up to its name because in those days of horses and carts it really was a foul ride in bad weather with no shelter from the wind or rain which used to sweep straight off the Downs and across it.

Up to quite comparatively recent years, commoners had grazing rights over this area of the "Green". One could see cattle being tended, or left tethered on this land. The road was narrow, following the same route as the present A22. Its traffic consisted mostly of the horse-drawn variety. Cars, were still few and far between. It was the duty of those tending the cattle to keep them from straying on to the road. This they had plenty of time to do, if the cattle decided to meander from the green on one side to that on the other, "Time" was always on the side of those who tended them.

We are now fast approaching the northern boundary of the Parish, and have now reached the entrance to the Windmill at which stood a large old house at the side of which ran a lane leading to the Windmill also to the Watermill down on the mill stream and again leading to the Isolation Hospital (a dreaded place in those days).

Of the Mill, and here let us please give it its rightful name "WILLINGDON MILL" as shown on all early ordnance maps dating back to it being built in 1817. This mill during one period of its existence was always referred to as Mocketts Mill, after the family who owned and worked it for many years. Built for Joseph Seymour, then came the Mocketts, later on the Ovendens. First father and then son, the latter being its last miller.

My father and my uncle were among many of the local farmers who used this mill to have their corn milled. I was always fascinated, as a youngster, to go there with them on various occasions to watch this process. It was awe inspiring, the noise from the revolving mill stones doing the grinding. The perpetual swish from the revolving sweeps and the action of the great wooden driving shaft is something I shall always remember.

We, here in Willingdon, tend to forget that nearby down on the mill stream wending its way down from Wannock, also stood a water mill which, too, like the Windmill was in operation from 1817 to about the same time as the closure of the Windmill. When there was no or little wind, or at a time when the amount of corn to be milled could not be coped with, then the water mill went into operation. The mill pond was fed by the constant flow of the stream, and by opening a sluice the water was diverted on to the wheel and the operation of grinding the corn was set into motion, in a similar way to that of the windmill.

110

The reason for the name of the mill being changed from WILLINGDON MILL to Polegate Windmill came about by sheer coincidence.

In 1913 an artist painted a picture of the mill and submitted it to the well known London Publishing firm trading as The Medici Society. They were attracted by the subject and its quality and straightaway purchased it from the artist who had titled it "Polegate Mill". Copies of this painting were published in various forms including prints, and calendars, and these found their way into many homes both at home and as well as abroad, especially to our then "Overseas Colonies". From that time onwards it more and more became to be known as "POLEGATE MILL" and, has since 1939 stood within the boundaries of the Parish of Polegate.

Continuing down the lane beyond the mill one came to the Isolation Hospital, well away from any other habitation. In those days diphtheria and scarlet fever were unfortunately quite common and it was to this Isolation Hospital such sufferers were taken. Here again the horse-drawn ambulance was to be seen coming to collect the patient. It was, of course, only used in connection with the Isolation Hospital and on either side had a blue cross in a white circle to distinguish it.

Unlike the "Black Maria" it had the reverse affect on the children in the village, instead of running to it, in this case it was running away from it, such was the fear and dread that its association with the Isolation Hospital had upon them.

Coming away from the mill one then continued down the steep little hill towards the stream. This part of the old main road is now re-named Clement Lane, but was for many years known locally as Mocketts Hill, named after Mockett the miller at the Mill. This name remained up to the time that this small area was by-passed and straightened out at the construction and widening of the present A22. Here we come to the spot where the mill stream passes under the road once dividing the Parish of Willingdon from that of Polegate; its natural boundary for so many years.

SOME INTERESTING PERSONALITIES AND OCCUPATIONS – From a list dated 1882.

Parish Clerk… James Stevens

Post, Money Order and Telegraph Office and Savings Bank – Thomas Martin, receiver. Letters arrive from Hawkhurst at 5.45 a.m. and 1.30 p.m. despatched at 11.30 a.m. and 7.45 p.m.

County Police Station, William Love, Constable in charge. Relieving Officer, Edmund Catt.

Parochial Schools, with Master's residence and supported by voluntary contributions, Augustus A. Haylock – Master, Mrs. H.M. Haylock – Infants Mistress.

Insurance Agent (County Fire and Life) Henry Alfred Hutchings.

Private Residents

Beever Henry "Shortlands"

Brown George

Catt Edmund, Junr.

Collins Wm. "Orchard Cottage"

Denham Mrs. "Spring Villa"

Fielder John "Park Farm"

Gosden James

Long Cecil "The Hoo"

Lowe Rev. Thomas M.A. The Vicarage

Lowe Harry, The Vicarage

Manser James Marchant James, Junr.

Mure Miss "Buckingham Lodge"

Perfect Miss "Shortlands"

Read George

Robinson William

Rudd James "Hockington House"

Seymour John Sampson

Thomas Mrs. M., "Ratton Park"

Willoughby Mrs.

Commercial

Baker Edgar Harry, Miller

Bean Albert Gearing, Beer Retailer, Pevensey Road

Bradford, David, Farmer Downs Farm

Carter Chas. Farmer, Lr. Willingdon

Catt Stephen & Matthias, Wheelwrights Lr Willingdon

Catt Edmund, Relieving Officer (Westham· District) The Butts

Carter William, Farmer

Catt Edmund Junr. Surveyor, Clerk to the Guardians of Hailsham Union and Clerk to the Arlington & Westham Board Schools Collector & Assistant Overseer for the Parish of Folkington, Pevensey, Westham, Willingdon and Wilmington – Church St. Willingdon.

Chapman Luke, Farmer

Climpson Charles, Farmer

Cooper Thomas, Farmer, "Hill Farm"

Cox Thomas, Beer Retailer

Darlington Fredk. A. Manager of the Eastbourne Gas Works

Dennis Charles, Market Gardener

Duly Tom, Shoeing & Jobbing Smith, Locksmith & Bellhanger, Gas & Hot Water Engineer and at Polegate.

East Sussex Book Hawking Association. (Fredk. Clarke, Traveller) Lr. Willingdon

Ellis Edward, Beer Retailer, Pevensey Road

French Frederick James, Grocer & Provision Dealer, Tobacconist, Plumber, Painter & Glazier, House Decorator, Gas & Hot Water Fitter, Lr. Willingdon.

Hall Harry, Farm Bailiff to J . Filder Esq.

Hilton Robert, Cow Keeper

Hollis Wm., Bailiff to Ratton Park Estate

Hutchings John Louis & Henry Alfred – Grocers and Drapers

Marchant James, Farmer

Markham George, Fly Proprietor.

Measey Philip, Beer Retailer, Lr. Willingdon.

Martin Thos. Builder, Contractor and Repairer of House Property – Post Office.

Mewett Frank Red Lion, Commercial Inn

Mewett George, Farmer, "Rippingtons"

Mewett James, Farmer

Miller James, Boot & Shoe Maker

Mockett Edwin Builders, General Ironmonger

Mockett Matthias, Miller & Farmer

Oxley James,Home made Bread Pastry Cook and Confectioner, deliveries in Eastbourne daily

Paxton John, Farmer Chalk Farm

Pike Edward, Baker, New Willingdon

Putland Walter, Farmer Townland Farm

Read Jn. & Son, Dairymen & Farmers, Graziers

Seymore & Marchant Builders, Contractors, Undertakers, Wheelrights, Painters & Glaziers

Stevens Benjamin, Farmer, Meachants Farm

Stevens Daaniel, Carrier

Stevens Fanny (Miss) Agent for the sale of Brushes, Mats etc. made by the Blind

Taylor Thomas, Carpenter

Thomas George, Miller and at Wannock .

Timson Alfred, Cook, Tea Dealer, Fancy Bread & Biscuit Maker, Pastry Cook & Confectioner, Wedding and other Cakes to order

Vine Wm. Farmer, Grazier, Butcher, Cattle Dealer and Land Owner

Wood George, Lodge Inn, Crumbles

CONCLUSION

To finalise these recollections of Old Willingdon, I feel that a fitting conclusion to them will be for me to quote a further poem from the pen of Miss Eva Parris, entitled "Our Village" . Eva Paris, bred and born in Willingdon has lived the whole of her life in that same cottage opposite the Village Pump. These were formerly Ratton Estate cottages, recorded in the Estate Register as 29 The Bank (but now 93 Wish Hill).

Eva's father was an employee of the Estate. He was one, whose duty it was to sound the bell in the bell tower at the Home Farm Rattan in order to summon the Estate workers to and from their work.

Eva Parris has been in charge of the Willingdon Church Sunday School for the last 45 years. She is now teaching the children of parents she once taught in their childhood days. What could be more fitting than to close this book with her delightful poem.

OUR VILLAGE

A little village at the foot of the Downs
On the main road to London Town,
A cottage here, a church on a hill,
The church is the same, it stands there still.

The farms, the pond, and the village Pound,
Meadows and corn and fallow ground,
A little school and the Wheatsheaf Inn,
And Flowershows at Ratton with cups to win.

Children with hoops and skipping ropes,
And the Sheep all grazing on Butts Brow slopes,
We wander to Hamlands round Huggetts Lane,
Over to Jordans and back again.

Up to the Home Farm after school,
To fetch the milk, each can so full,
We stand it carefully on the old stone wall,
While we shake a bough 'till the walnuts fall.

The village street, with men filling pails,
At the village pump, and telling tales,
Children tired at the end of the day,
On the top of a wagon-load of hay.

For today they have cut the chapel field,
And the farmer is proud of his fragrant yield,
The great old carthorse lumbers along,
And the evening air is filled with song.

Nobody's yet heard of Willingdon Way,
Or Chichester Close, those are fields where we play,
Where's Summerlands Road? I really don't know,
Oh! you mean down there, where the blackberries grow.

Where is Willingdon Trees?
Where is Winchester Way?
These are the questions we are asked today,

For the fields are all gone and farms are sold,
And everywhere there is change to behold.

Many new roads and many new homes,
Pretty new gardens, gay borders and gnomes,
A shopping precinct and a subway too,
And the By-Pass takes the traffic through.

But we still have the downs and we still have the view
Though the farmlands have gone and the meadows too
In their place Anderida and Babylon Way, '
And the Hamlands Estate has come to stay.

There's Walnut Tree Walk where our walnut trees stood
And beautiful houses in Ratton Wood,
This little village at the foot of the Downs,
On the main road to London Town,
It's still our village as of yore,
Let's keep it this way for evermore.

Eva Parris.

Printed in Great Britain
by Amazon